Words That Work In Business

A Practical Guide to Effective Communication in the Workplace

2nd Edition

By Ike Lasater

With Julie Stiles

PuddleDancer
PRESS

2240 Encinitas Blvd., Ste. D-911, Encinitas, CA 92024
email@PuddleDancer.com • www.PuddleDancer.com

For additional information:
Center for Nonviolent Communication
9301 Indian School Rd., NE, Suite 204, Albuquerque, NM 87112
Ph: 505-244-4041 • Fax: 505-247-0414 • Email: cnvc@cnvc.org • Website: www.cnvc.org

Words That Work In Business, 2nd Edition
A Practical Guide to Effective Communication in the Workplace

PuddleDancer Press, Permissions Dept.
2240 Encinitas Blvd., Ste. D-911, Encinitas, CA 92024
Tel: 760-652-5754 Fax: 760-274-6400
www.NonviolentCommunication.com Email@PuddleDancer.com

Ordering Information
Please contact Independent Publishers Group, Tel: 312-337-0747;
Fax: 312-337-5985; Email: frontdesk@ipgbook.com or visit www.IPGbook.com
for other contact information and details about ordering online

Author: Ike Lasater
Contributor: Julie Stiles
Editor: Kyra Freestar
Indexer: Beth Nauman-Montana
Cover and Interior Design: Shannon Bodie, Lightbourne.com
Cover source photo: www.istock.com

Manufactured in the United States of America,
1st Printing, March 2010, 2nd Printing, March 2019
♻ Printed on recycled paper.

23 22 21 20 19   1 2 3 4 5

ISBN: 978-1-934336-15-1

Library of Congress Cataloging-in-Publication Data

Names: Lasater, Ike, author. | Stiles, Julie, author.
Title: Words that work in business : a practical guide to effective
    communication in the workplace / by Ike Lasater with Julie Stiles.
Description: 2nd Edition. | Encinitas, CA : PuddleDancer Press, [2018] |
    Revised edition. | Includes bibliographical references and index.
Identifiers: LCCN 2018035905| ISBN 9781934336151 (trade paper : alk. paper) |
    ISBN 9781934336274 (ebook pdf) | ISBN 9781934336335 (mobi/kindle)
Subjects: LCSH: Business communication. | Communication in organizations. |
    Interpersonal relations.
Classification: LCC HF5718 .L37 2018 | DDC 651.7--dc23
LC record available at https://lccn.loc.gov/2018035905

Endorsements of *Words That Work In Business*

"Creating workplaces that serve their purpose in line with their values is a tall order. Ultimately, systemic change would be needed, both in the world at large and within organizations themselves. Yet, what *Words That Work in Business* shows, with lively examples and accessible language, is that a lot more collaboration is possible even when the larger organization is not set up to collaborate. It's refreshing to see how much more is possible than we often imagine when we focus on clear, effective, honest, and caring communication."

—MIKI KASHTAN, Lead facilitator and trainer, Bay Area Nonviolent
Communication (BayNVC); Lead Collaboration Consultant, Center for
Efficient Collaboration, Author, *Reweaving Our Human Fabric:
Working Together to Create a Nonviolent Future*

"When I was new to Nonviolent Communication, I was enthused to find *Words That Work in Business* by Ike Lasater. It gave me encouragement and practical guidelines on how to integrate NVC in collaboration with my colleagues. The first edition of the book was very helpful in learning the skill of silent empathy. I was thrilled to read the second edition and find the helpful new chapter with practical small steps for daily work life. I recommend this book for everybody longing to create a fulfilling work environment."

—GÜNTHER MILD, Psychiatrist and psychotherapist,
Germany Founder, Center for Peace and Connection
(a Meditation and Mediation Training Center)
www.theheartpilgrim.org

"If I had a boss this is the kind of book that I would like her to read. With its aim to help us be the best human beings we can be and make work life both productive and meaningful, I would recommend it to anyone. I love the skills combined with examples so that I can understand the concepts in a real-world setting of people working together. This book captures so much more than just words."

—LIV LARSSON, NVC trainer and mediator, Author, *Reclaiming Power
and Choice: Handling Anger, Guilt,* and *Shame and A Helping Hand:
Mediation with Nonviolent Communication*

"*Words That Work In Business* offers helpful tips, insights, and anecdotes to help you get up to speed in using NVC at work. The book includes the practice of silent empathy and inspiring stories about a lawyer integrating NVC in the courtroom (perhaps one of the most challenging environments to practice NVC, given power-over dynamics), plus a helpful section on addressing challenging workplace situations. Valuable to anyone wanting to deepen their empathy practice in colloquial ways."

—Dian Killian, PhD, CNVC Certified Trainer and
coauthor of *Connecting Across Differences*

"Bring focus and peace to work: Ike's practical exercises help you better understand and control your communication style. The step-by-step process helps you build trust and confidence in your professional environment and become a more thoughtful coworker."

—ALEXIA OHANNESSIAN, Working remotely for Trello

"Nonviolent Communication (NVC) offers a way of using language and awareness that goes to the heart of how we connect as human beings and how we can work together to make a better world. Ironically however, these powerful insights can be inadvertently practiced in ways that are counter-productive. *Words That Work in Business* provides invaluable guidance and practical suggestions on how to use NVC in ways that bring out its full transformational potential, particularly in the organizational world. If you practice what is in this book it will change your life and your workplace."

—JOHN KINYON, CNVC, trainer and cofounder of
Mediate Your Life training, coaching, and mediation,
Author, *From Conflict to Connection: Transforming
Difficult Conversations Into Peaceful Resolutions*,
https://www.mediateyourlife.com/

Contents

Preface

Six Steps to Freedom

first met Marshall Rosenberg, the developer of Nonviolent Communication (NVC), at a workshop in May of 1996. We met for three days, twenty-five or so of us, for an introductory training. We covered the basics—Observations, Feelings, Needs, and Requests. I was exhilarated; such a simple model that explained so much. Many of us, including myself, were deeply touched during the workshop.

On the evening of the second day, I was having dinner with Judith, my wife of twenty-four years, and our three children, ages nineteen, sixteen, and fourteen. In my enthusiasm, I remember telling them what I had learned, then, soon after, correcting someone who had tried to apply what I had just related. I said, in a sharp voice, "That's not a feeling!" My reaction indicated to me how much there was to learn and how ingrained the patterns were that I wanted to replace. Since then, the phrase "That's not a feeling" has become my private NVC joke I tell on myself.

In learning NVC, I found out how easy it was to take on a new rule set and apply it in the paradigm in which I already lived. I had been socialized into a way of being, first at my mother's breast, and then in the rough-and-tumble of the shame-and-blame world of my peers. I had learned to adapt and, at times, to thrive in that paradigm and in the societal systems it pervades. Years later when I reviewed my notes from that first workshop with Marshall, I chuckled to see how I had twisted his words into rules, like "Don't say it this way . . ." and "You should say . . ." and so forth.

I recount this history in part because it is what I do not want for you. I do not want you, in the celebration of discovery, to do what I found so easy—which was to foist my own sense of NVC on other people before I had worked it into my being. I know firsthand the suffering that can be created. What I want for you is the following: if you find something useful in this book, for you to apply it in your own life before you try to interest anyone else in it. Make requests of yourself and others, not demands. Learn the difference. Feel the difference. Learn to learn. This is what I still want most for myself—and thus also for you.

I have found NVC is in part a way of remaking my perception of reality by how I think and speak about it, and is in part an approach, heavily dependent on the use of language, for mediating my interactions with others. Thus, NVC is not only about how I use language to communicate with myself (i.e., how I think) and with others (i.e., how I speak), but about how I filter my perception of the sensory inputs from the world inside and outside of me. NVC has been very helpful for me as a tool, a strategy if you will, to live my values in the world. My emphasis here is on NVC being a strategy and not an end in and of itself.

As you read about NVC in this book, you may form the impression that I am referring to an established and concrete "system." I am not. Instead, I offer my sense of NVC, that is, my interpretation of my experiences. I encourage you to approach NVC as something to experiment with—not as a static thing, nor as a need in and of itself. Try out what I suggest, paying attention to your experiences as you do so. Learn what works for you. In this way, NVC will become a part of you, out of your self-discovered and self-appropriated learning.

To the extent possible, I intend the interpretations in this book to be my own. My interpretations are based on years of workshops with Marshall Rosenberg and many others, and on applying what I have learned in a variety of contexts: mediating innumerable disputes, coaching people in conflicts, facilitating workshops, and serving six years on the board of the Center for Nonviolent Communication (CNVC). I have attempted to embody my understanding of NVC and apply it daily; in doing so, my presentation of NVC is altered from how it was presented to me. Consequently, in this writing, I make no claim that what I present as NVC corresponds with anyone else's interpretation.

Julie Stiles has been intimately involved in the writing and editing process, such that her views of the world have inevitably found their way into this text. From my vantage point, this inevitable part of our collaboration has made this book not only possible, but immensely better than it would have been otherwise.

Finally, I request your feedback regarding how we might improve this book in subsequent editions. Particularly, I would like to know what you think we have left out and how you think what we have included could be made better. If you are willing to provide this feedback, please email me at ikelasater@me.com.

Introduction

I wrote the first edition of this book, with coauthor Julie Stiles, about ten years ago. In the years since, I have continued to facilitate people in challenging situations to be heard as they would like to be and hear others as they would like as well. I have trained people in more than twenty countries to do the same, thereby deepening my own understanding and integration of the skills offered in this book, and I expanded my capacity to use those skills in emotionally charged, high-stakes, high-conflict situations. As I reviewed *Words That Work in Business* with the idea of publishing a second edition, what struck me was how relevant it still is.

In some ways, *Words That Work in Business* was ahead of its time, as perhaps all of Nonviolent Communication has been. The ideas in this book are becoming more mainstream, with increased coverage in the media and research on such topics as empathy, positive psychology, happiness, and meaning in the workplace.

Often in the workplace, the focus is on the actual work being done. Yet, the underpinning of all efforts in any industry is communication. The key to successful communication is connection. Without self-connection, you are not going to stay present and focused on your priorities. Without connection to the person you are speaking to, you might as well save your breath, because the other person will not be available to your influence in a way that you will like.

This book—and all of my work—is fundamentally about having the tools to evaluate these conversations, including whether they are moving us in the direction we want. For instance, we have a conversation and then debrief how it went in order to learn from it. We decide how we want to do it differently next time, and eventually, we have that next conversation. This learning cycle repeats itself again and again, each iteration getting us closer to creating what we want. In this way, we create our lives one conversation at a time, whether in our personal or professional lives. All efforts to succeed in any endeavor occur in this way.

The measure we encourage using in this learning cycle is *needs:* Did what just happened meet your needs, or when looking to the future, do you predict that one strategy versus another will better meet your needs? When you are consistently assessing and acting to meet your needs, you experience increased satisfaction and meaning in your life. With that, you're more effective in contributing to others' well-being.

Popular culture is catching up to this idea that contribution, satisfaction, meaning, and happiness are important and worth paying attention to in the workplace. Yet, despite this increased attention to these topics, the "how" of creating these outcomes is often lacking.

Words That Work In Business provides that "how." It tells you where to focus your attention and what conduct to engage in—what to say and do—in challenging workplace situations. I've come to realize that these are the only two things over which you have some conscious control.

When I am in a challenging situation and flooded with emotion, having a map that I have practiced is like a port in a storm. A map tells me what to pay attention to and what to do. It guides me through the shoals of my conflict habits when they would otherwise take over my thoughts and actions. How often do we look back on such situations and regret what we have said and done? Practicing the skills necessary to execute these maps helps us to step out of our conflict habits and to reduce the regret we so often experience for what we have said and done under the powerful sway of the stress hormones that flood us with emotion.

Of course, my thinking has evolved during the ten years since I first wrote this book, and if you're familiar with my more recent books, including *Choosing Peace, From Conflict to Connection,* and *When Your Mind Sabotages Your Dreams,* you'll see that evolution. Yet despite how my understanding has grown, the skills, concepts, and practices included in *Words That Work in Business* are still relevant and accurate. Hence, I haven't tried to rewrite this book to be entirely consistent with the language used in later works.

New in this edition is a series of Workplace Communication Tips, which are included in Chapter 7. We'll discuss both where these came from and how you can use them to enhance your integration of the skills in these pages in the introduction to the tips beginning on page 109.

I have also written a companion to *Words That Work in Business*, titled *Collaborating in the Workplace: A Guide for Building Better Teams*, that provides specific maps to support people working in teams, whether in the workplace or in the community. These maps guide you through conversations, both with yourself and others, and provide the groundwork to produce the outcomes you want.

Perhaps what has become clearest to me since the first edition was published is the importance of practicing the skills it explores in order to integrate them easily and habitually into day-to-day life. The clarity of this insight arose early on in my learning journey when many times I had the skills at my disposal but, in specific emotionally charged moments, did not have the capacity to actually use those skills. Much of my learning and offering of trainings to others has focused on how to develop this capacity to use these skills when flooded with emotion.

Finally, I have found the strategies offered in this book have transformed, much for the better, how I go about living my life. I hope they change your life for the better as well.

Chapter 1

Can I *Really* Use NVC in My Workplace?

Some of you may have had the following experience. Having just emerged from a Nonviolent Communication workshop, full of possibilities and hopes, you feel energized and excited to have meaningful, connected communications. In your enthusiasm to share what you have learned, you go home or back to work, and the first chance you get, you try out something from the workshop. Instead of the powerful emotional connection and intimate response you were hoping for, the person says, "Why are you talking like that?" You feel your excitement fade, your energy sink, and to your chagrin, you find yourself reacting as you normally do instead of in the compassionate, connected way you imagined.

When our initial attempts to practice or share what we have learned are met with a not-so-enthusiastic reception, these experiences sometimes lead us to believe that the new skills will be difficult to apply in certain situations—such as in the workplace. Thus, while you have begun learning about NVC and might already have found its value for yourself, you may have thought something like this: "I can see the value of NVC in my personal life, and maybe some people can use it in their workplaces, but no way at my work! The people in my workplace just wouldn't be open to it!"

I can understand these thoughts, since I have had them too. When I first began learning NVC, I was working as a trial lawyer.

The last lawsuit I tried (in 1999, just prior to withdrawing from the practice of law and beginning to serve on the board of the Center for Nonviolent Communication) was a United States federal court case in the Central Valley of California. The case concerned the dumping of toxic agricultural chemicals. One of the government witnesses was a well-qualified analytical chemist who had never before testified in court. I knew her testimony because I had taken her deposition, and during the trial I wanted to highlight certain aspects of it to make sure they went into the court record. My cross-examination quickly turned into a painful and unpleasant process. When I would ask a question, she would answer the question—but then take time to unnecessarily restate all the aspects of her opinion that she had already testified to.

In my frustration, I began to use the many techniques I had been trained in as a lawyer to try to control her and get her to stop these long, duplicative explanations. None of these techniques worked. In fact, we found out during a break that she had interpreted my attempts as trying to demean her. With some embarrassment, I report to you that it did not occur to me the whole day to attempt a different way to communicate.

I was distressed about this situation; we were already over our estimated schedule, and I was concerned the judge would cut off the cross-examination if it continued in the same way. That evening, as I pondered what I could do, a small voice in my head said, "You could try NVC."

Immediately, my response was, "No, not in this situation!" My training and experience in the stilted environment of the courtroom— me at a lectern, the witness in the witness box, the judge on the bench, and a number of opposing attorneys all ready to object to any language that deviated from their expectations—made it difficult for me to see how I could apply the skills I was learning. Nonetheless, in my distress, I began considering how I might go about using NVC. After a time of empathizing with myself, I found myself practicing conversations with the witness in my head.

The following day, the pattern started again, with my questions and the witness's long, repetitive answers. So I interrupted her, and when I had her attention, I said: "I'm concerned about the time it's going to take to complete your testimony. I'm wondering if you would be willing to just answer my questions and save any explanation you have until later. I want to assure you that you will have time to consult with government counsel before your testimony is complete, and that you will be able to provide further explanations. For now, would you be willing to just answer my questions?"

Now, as I was asking this question, my heart was racing. I felt it in my throat. To this day, I am not clear on what I was telling myself that stimulated this reaction. Perhaps I was terrified that someone was going to object, "You can't use NVC in the courtroom!" Of course, no one did. The moment passed, and after looking to government counsel for confirmation, the witness agreed to my request. Though I had to remind her of her agreement a couple times, overall the cross-examination proceeded much more quickly and smoothly.

My intense, physical reaction to attempting a new way of communicating highlights the difficulty that many of us face when trying to shift our behavior within an established environment. We believe the people around us expect us to act a certain way, and often we react to this by confining our behavior and communication within the narrow bounds of our beliefs about their expectations. There is a way out of this.

If you have found that introducing something new to your workplace is fraught with uncertainty and angst, this book is intended for you. The suggestions in this book can be applied to all areas of your life; nevertheless, the focus is on the workplace, as people often feel uncomfortable trying new communication skills with coworkers, managers, and employees. This can particularly be the case when people are not confident that their needs for sustainability and survival will continue to be met in the work situation.

Yet these work relationships, as much as other relationships, stand to benefit from your NVC knowledge—and we hope your enjoyment of work will increase as a result. We start with the premise that you will be able to use aspects of your NVC skills in the workplace no matter what your skill level. We suggest a set of skills and ways to practice that will build your confidence in your NVC fluency to the point where you will be able to apply what you have learned even in situations where, right now, you have little trust in ever being comfortable using NVC out loud.

A Few Notes Before We Begin

These pages are designed to deepen the learning you have already begun, with the goal that you can comfortably use your Nonviolent Communication skills in your workplace. Before going into the second chapter, we offer some reminders about NVC that will give context for the rest of the book. In Chapter 2, we will explore practicing NVC silently. This way, you can begin applying your skills immediately, even in situations where you might feel uncomfortable doing so aloud. Chapter 3 explains the cycle of learning and its relationship to mourning and celebration practices. These practices can be especially important as a means of reminding you of your desire to expand your communication skills and of the commitments you have made to yourself to do so. Since practice is key to fully integrating skills into your life, Chapter 4 is devoted to exploring ways to practice that will support your intentions. We see making requests as a crucial part of NVC practice and one that few of us seem to have mastered, so in Chapter 5, we will discuss how to make requests that are more likely to meet your needs. Finally, for when you have begun to solidify your skills and are looking for additional challenges, the last chapter gives examples for dealing with typical workplace issues.

We encourage you to use this book in several ways. If you decide to read it through to the end, we encourage you to take time along the way to experience the practice suggestions. Alternatively, you may want to pick a chapter that discusses a current problem you are facing. For example, if you find yourself in a conflict at work and notice you have judgments about yourself or the other people involved, you might want to go to the enemy image section in Chapter 6, "Suggestions for Addressing Common Workplace Communication Challenges."

You may be inclined to simply read a book such as this one without practicing anything. To encourage you to practice, boxes titled "Practice Pause" are placed throughout the text. We hope that these exercises will entice you to stop reading and practice—right then and there—before continuing further. We want the Practice Pauses to remind you that every moment is potentially a practice moment.

There are also examples throughout the text drawn from workplace situations, in which the protagonist ("you") interacts with a boss, Magna, and two coworkers, Harold and Karen. These examples give additional illustrations of how to work with the language and intention of NVC in real-life situations. Because of limitations of the written word and space, the examples may give a false impression of the real-life process of empathy, and particularly its quality of wandering in your pondering before reaching a point of clarity about needs (one's own or others'). Thus, we encourage you to get what value you can from these examples without believing that the empathy process will be as quick, easy, or linear as the written scenarios may seem to suggest.

Reminders

In the early stages of learning, Nonviolent Communication can appear to be about word choice and order—in other words, syntax—and we will focus most of our attention on these aspects. While doing this, we would like you to bear in mind that fundamentally NVC is about intention; the syntax is, first, a strategy to remind us of our intention and, second, a way to make our intention more readily heard by others. The underlying intention in using NVC is to connect—for each of us to connect with ourselves and with others. Out of this connection, we can create mutually satisfying outcomes. With our intention clearly in mind, we are freed to adapt the actual words we use to fit in with the situation or subculture we find ourselves in. For example, in this book we will talk about needs in a particular way—typically when attempting to identify a universal human need in one word. In direct communication with another person, however, what is important is the intention to connect; the words are secondary to that end. In these situations, we hope you will use words that have meaning and resonance for the person with whom you are talking, and that at the same time identify needs (i.e., universal human needs that are not specific to a particular strategy).

At the heart of the intention to connect is being connected—in a visceral, noncognitive way—with yourself, which is to say with your own needs. This is not something most of us are taught as children. We begin as children to form habitual reaction patterns, which become ingrained with time as we continue to react habitually.

Learning to connect at the level of needs is a way to step out of these habitual ways of reacting, yet is something that generally takes time and practice to develop. As we identify, time and time again, the needs that were and were not met by our actions, particularly in situations where we reacted habitually, space opens within us to act differently in the future. In this way, in continually returning to being present and connecting with needs, we alter how we relate to ourselves and others. We contribute to creating a world more in alignment with our values.

When we make it a practice to connect with our needs, we shift into learning mode. For example, let's say you react habitually to a coworker's remark. Afterward, you realize that your reaction was not in harmony with your values. At this point, you might inquire into the need you were seeking to meet by your reaction, as well as what needs of yours were not met. The natural result of this inquiry is the question, "How might I do it differently next time to better meet my needs?" This entire inquiry we encourage you to do without a sense of judgment, punishment, blame, shame, guilt, anger, or depression: instead, simply realize what needs were and were not met, and seek new ways to better meet them. When you do this often, you create a cyclical learning process of becoming aware, mourning and celebrating your conduct, and building on what you liked or shifting away from what you didn't like, all in order to meet your needs (see Chapter 3 for more on this learning cycle). Soon, you begin to remember in the moment and try new choices, and then you learn from those choices. The natural consequence of this process is learning skills that are in alignment with the intention to meet your needs and the needs of others.

This is not the process I learned during childhood and socialization into the adult world. I was implicitly taught how to analyze who was at fault, and thus who was to be blamed and punished. I learned how to protect myself from criticism, avoid punishment, and redirect blame. The results of this not-very-conscious process of blame and shame determined how I felt. My learning was how to avoid being blamed and punished; thus, I learned to avoid what I did not want. This process did not help me learn what would enable me to flourish and thrive or how to create the life I wanted. In making the shift to connecting with needs, I identify the needs that I yearn to be meeting and therefore liberate my mind to do what it does well, which is to sift through the patterns of experience to identify strategies that might meet my needs. I enter a cycle of learning how to create what I want.

Thus, from my perspective, the core of being able to use NVC in the workplace is not only developing the skills and practicing, but also learning to choose new possibilities based on a connection with needs instead of repeating deeply rooted habitual patterns. By being connected with our own needs, our intention is clarified moment by moment.

The specific syntax you learn with NVC was designed to help you uncover your intention and remember it in the moment. I've found in my own experience and in working with others that there is a stage of learning in which using the basic NVC sentence can be extremely valuable (see Appendix A for examples). I call this the *training wheels sentence*: "When I hear . . . , I feel . . . , because I need . . . Would you be willing to . . . ?" My hypothesis is that people who skip this stage take longer to really embody the perspective-altering potential of NVC, if they ever do. This may be because they have not ingrained the basic distinctions that using the training wheels sentence over and over again seems to cultivate. The four basic NVC distinctions that I am referring to are Observations versus judgments, Feelings versus evaluations masquerading as feelings, Needs versus strategies, and Requests versus demands. These distinctions are embedded in the structure of the training wheels sentence, and thus using the sentence prompts awareness of them. Practicing the training wheels sentence is the only way I have found to get these basic distinctions at a deep level, as the sentence encourages us to focus on each of the four parts of communication—Observations, Feelings, Needs, and Requests.

When these distinctions are embodied, and you are clear that your intention is to connect (with yourself or another person), the specific words you use become less important. On the other hand, people often report early on that they are using all the "right" words, but are not getting the results they expect—this may be because they are not yet consistent in their intention.

The premise of NVC is that when you focus on connection with yourself and others, you will be meeting your needs while, at the same time, others in your world are meeting their needs. We often believe that if we can analyze a situation properly, then we will get what we want. NVC suggests instead that when we are connected to needs, all of us can be in the process of meeting our needs.

NVC is simple, but not easy. At least, that is my experience, and others have reported the same. In the beginning, it is particularly difficult to remember these new ideas in the moment. Since NVC is as much a consciousness—a way of thinking about and approaching our communication with others—as it is a set of skills, adults socialized into mainstream culture find there is much "unlearning" that happens as we begin to integrate the NVC we have learned. In the moment when we are communicating with someone, our old learning is initially going to be stronger than our new learning. The goal of this book is to show you some ways to strengthen your new learning so you can incorporate NVC into all parts of your life, and in particular, your work life.

Chapter 2

How to Begin: Silent NVC Practices

You may be feeling some trepidation about using Nonviolent Communication in the workplace. Perhaps you imagine that coworkers will respond negatively if you attempt to introduce a new way of communicating. Yet there is almost nothing a person can say or do that cannot be responded to either with empathy or with some form of self-connected expression, or a combination of the two. When you begin to trust that you will predictably have the skills and presence to respond with empathy or expression, you'll have more trust in your ability to interact in ways that are in alignment with your values. Often, however, people see this as a chicken-and-egg problem: How do I get the skills if I'm afraid to use them? How do I use them without having the skills? A powerful way to develop NVC skills is through silent practice. This section covers three silent practices—awareness of blocking connection, self-empathy, and silent empathy—and suggests when and how you might use them.

There are several benefits to silent NVC practice: you can practice in ways less likely to be noticed by others in your workplace; you can practice and develop your skills of self-empathy and silent empathy until you feel more confident trying the out loud skills of empathy and expression; and finally, whatever you do say after silent practice will probably be something you like.

The inner work of NVC can be done without anyone knowing.

Though silent, these practices produce empathic connection with yourself and with others. When connected in this way, you will be a different person, and you will be more likely to enjoy your conduct. In addition, what you say and how you say it will be affected, even though you are not yet intending to use out loud NVC. These subtle changes create a gradual process that will help you transition to using out loud skills with coworkers who might otherwise react to a sudden change in your communication.

Becoming Aware of Blocking Connection

Many of the ways we have learned to communicate result in blocking connection with others. If you intend to use Nonviolent Communication to create connection with yourself or others, we encourage you to become aware, simultaneously, of what you are doing that blocks that connection. To gain this self-awareness, we suggest a two-step process.

First, notice the times when you feel less than connected while speaking with someone. You might notice a vague feeling of discomfort, realize you do not enjoy what you or they are saying, or feel angry or impatient. (See Example 1 on facing page.)

Second, when you notice you are not feeling as connected as you would like, determine whether either of you are doing any of the following: defending a position, explaining, moralistically judging, diagnosing others, blaming, seeking to punish, or "needing" to be right. Any internal sense of wanting the other to feel guilt or shame also tends to generate disconnection.

Your awareness of blocking connection will come over time as you look at the results from your communication. One thing to watch for is that you do not, in the process of gaining this awareness, continue to block connection by judging or blaming or punishing yourself for not having communicated "right." In a learning process, there is no "right" or "wrong"; there is only learning—inquiry that leads to trying something else designed to better meet your needs. Likewise, we warn against using your developing awareness to name what those around you are doing. For instance, if you can, refrain from saying things like "There you go again, defending your position" or "Stop trying to guilt-trip me." Instead, trust that as your awareness grows, you will be able to use your expanding out loud NVC skills of empathy or expression to respond to what others say.

Awareness is always the first part of a learning process, and the silent practice of becoming aware of blocking connection is crucial for learning to quickly recognize the patterns of communication you hope to change.

Example 1

Karen, your colleague, comes into your office one day to discuss the project you are both working on. She says, "You know, we have this big meeting coming up, and I'm concerned about being prepared for it." You respond: "Yes, I know I have let some things slip, but I've been really overwhelmed between this project and the other things on my plate already. I've already put in so much extra time, and partly the holdup is because of Harold not getting the numbers to me on time." After a couple more exchanges, Karen leaves your office. You realize that the conversation didn't go as you would have liked. You didn't feel connected to Karen nor did you feel that she understood your situation. In remembering your response to her initial statement of concern, you realize that defending, explaining, and blaming all slipped easily into your communication.

Using Self-Empathy—Recognizing Your Triggers

We often get triggered while interacting with others. The stimulus may arise from something someone else said, or something we did or said ourselves. Without awareness, a trigger leads us into habitual reaction. From the moment of awareness, however, we can choose to intervene, to create an alternative to the habitual. With time, if we prefer the outcomes from this alternative and continue to reinforce them, we will develop new reaction habits. The intervention we suggest is self-empathy. (See Example 2 on facing page.)

In self-empathy, we practice the basics of NVC within ourselves—silently. We identify what was actually said or done—the observation of the situation—and distinguish that from our judgment of it. Then we identify how we feel about it, and what need was or was not met by the words or actions. In my work as a trainer and mediator, I use self-empathy all the time. I find it essential for maintaining my sense of well-being and wholeness.

For instance, not long ago I was facilitating a workshop. There had been several joking exchanges between myself and people I knew well from previous workshops. One of the participants who was new to this group then said, "I'm really uncomfortable with all this joking; it's not at all what I consider to be NVC, and my understanding is that this is supposed to be an NVC workshop."

As soon as I heard her say this, I immediately noticed that I felt de-energized and that I was thinking thoughts like "Well, you're a real party-pooper." Realizing these two things prompted me to ask myself what need I was seeking to meet with a thought like that. What occurred to me was that I wanted to have the freedom to be myself and for that to be OK. I also wanted to have companionship in my fun and play. With this awareness, I felt a shift within me to a sense of compassion in myself and for her. From this shift, I was able to respond to her with care and understanding about what might have prompted her to say what she said.

There are often a number of different ways to proceed with

self-empathy. For instance, in the story above, I could have started with either the observation of what the participant said or the observation of the judgment I heard in my mind. I began with my judgment, to give myself empathy first for having reacted in that way. Alternatively, I might have started with how I felt or with a direct guess about my needs. The point is that my goal was self-connection through the strategy of identifying my needs.

Example 2

In a meeting with the rest of your project team, as you are describing where you are on your part of the project, Harold says, "Let's see if we can keep this part of the meeting to fifteen minutes, shall we?" You leave the meeting angry, thinking that he interrupted you and that his remark was directed at you. As you go back to your office, you close the door and decide to practice some self-empathy. You think, "He interrupted and said I was taking too much time," then realize that thought is a judgment, not an observation. You rephrase it as an observation: "He began speaking when I was speaking, and said . . ." As you reflect more upon your anger, you realize that you also feel hurt, because your need for respect and to be heard in the group was not met. As you get in touch with your needs for respect and to be heard, you feel an opening in your chest, and the heaviness that you've been feeling lifts.

Although there are multiple entry points for connecting with yourself through the process of self-empathy, I am particularly struck by the power of the role of needs. When I shift my perspective from

"He made me sad" to observation and needs language—"When I hear him say that, I feel sad because I need consideration"—I more accurately describe my internal experience in relation to what I perceive occurring outside of me at that moment. The sentence "He made me sad" suggests that "he" is the one with control: he can cause me to feel sad; I am powerless to be other than sad. When I use this language, I give up my power to dictate my reactions—my feelings. On the other hand, when I say, "When I see him do that, I feel sad *because* I need consideration," I am saying I know why I am sad, and his conduct is only the start of the story, not in and of itself the reason I am experiencing what I am experiencing. The use of "because" reminds me (and others) that I understand my sadness arises out of my needs and my interpretation of his conduct, and it avoids blaming the other person.

Moreover, when I use a language of observations and needs, I communicate what has happened to me as the result of my observation. The "because" leaves open the possibility that others observing the same conduct might have completely different reactions. Haven't you watched a movie with friends and found that some of you cried, others did not? You watched and listened to the same movie. But because each of us has had different life experiences, each of us views the world from a different perspective.

With my language, I can signal that my internal state—my reactions—are not at the mercy of another person's conduct. Yes, I am reacting with sadness now. However, that is the result of *my* internal processes. If my sense of internal well-being were dependent upon the other person conforming their conduct so that I would not feel sad next time I saw them under similar circumstances, I would not be particularly hopeful. However, I am hopeful when I think that my sadness results from my interpretations, because I can affect my interpretation process over time. Self-empathy has helped me do just that.

As you begin practicing self-empathy, you may find it helpful to get support from somebody else to help you to formulate your observations, and to identify your feelings and needs, especially if you are not skilled yet in identifying your needs. Another person can help you meet your need for empathy by guessing your feelings and needs. This can be helpful even if it takes place some time after the stimulus. Working with a person familiar with the process of connecting with needs has another benefit. Through their guesses, you can begin to experience the physiological shift that often takes place when you connect deeply with a need; this shift might be a release, a feeling of opening or lightening, or perhaps simply a deepening of your emotional response.

If you do not have another person to practice with, you can use other techniques to feel that physiological shift. When you have identified what you think might be the need not met in a situation, imagine internally what it would feel like for that need to be met. For example, if the need you identified is consideration, go into a kind of reverie where you imagine that your need for consideration is met; what does that feel like in your body? This is a way of deepening into what it feels like to be in touch with a need. When you are in touch with this feeling, you can then see if any strategies come to mind for meeting it. If none come to mind immediately, pay attention over the next day or so and see if any pop into your mind at unexpected moments. Trust that your mind is working on strategies even when you are not consciously thinking about it.

Practice Pause

Stop reading and check in with yourself right now. What are you feeling? What needs are behind that feeling? See if you can connect with at least one need.

Once you become familiar with your own typical somatic response to identifying your needs, you can use it in your self-empathy practice. This felt sense can be your guide and benchmark for when you have connected with a need you were trying to meet. Typically, this shift opens up a space for compassion, for yourself as well as for the other people involved.

Self-empathy is particularly powerful when we have the presence to use it in the moment when we realize we have been triggered (or as soon afterward as we can). It can also be used much later, if we find we still have an unwelcome reaction to the event, or even in anticipation of an interaction. If we are anticipating a difficult conversation with someone, we can practice self-empathy beforehand (perhaps again with another's help) to prepare and enter the conversation with the clarity that arises from clearly naming and thereby connecting with our needs. I recommend spending time each day in self-empathy (see Chapter 3 on mourning and celebration in the learning cycle).

I view self-empathy as the fundamental practice of NVC. Even if you did no other practice, consistently meeting your need for empathy would be life-changing in and of itself. You can increase your adeptness in self-empathy, as a key silent practice, by using it at work in a myriad of situations. Practice self-empathy silently when in meetings, when you find yourself triggered or upset at an interaction, when you realize you are not connected with your own needs, and in anticipation of, during, and after difficult conversations with coworkers, managers, or employees. As you use self-empathy, notice any changes in your thought process and in how you feel.

Using Silent Empathy—Understanding Your Coworkers

In general, when we are in pain and our thoughts are awhirl, we are not able to empathize with others until our need for empathy has been sufficiently met. Hence, self-empathy is an important first step in integrating Nonviolent Communication; once we are connected with ourselves, then we will be more interested in and curious about the other person. (See Example 3 on facing page.) At this point our attention and focus turns to them, and the question that typically arises is some version of "What is going on with them?" If we ask this question before having met our own need for empathy, our minds will typically jump to analyzing the other person's "wrongness" with thoughts like "None of this would have happened if he hadn't been such a jerk." When we are full of empathy, however, the question becomes "Which needs of theirs are they seeking to meet?" This inquiry leads right into the practice of silent empathy.

Example 3

Because you now feel lighter due to your connection with your own needs, you begin to wonder about what happened in the meeting. Was Harold really directing his comment at you? What need might he have been trying to meet in saying, "Let's see if we can keep this part of the meeting to fifteen minutes, shall we?" As you think back, you realize that Harold might have been meeting his need for consideration of his time and for integrity around agreements about time commitments. As you realize this, you experience a release of your antagonism toward Harold and you feel more accepting of him.

The process of silent empathy is the same as the process of self-empathy, except that you are internally inquiring about another person instead of yourself. You can use the four components of Observations, Feelings, Needs, and Requests to ask yourself what might have been going on from the other person's perspective, and we suggest you pay particular attention to needs. Essentially, you are guessing what is going on with the other person without checking those guesses with them. Silent empathy can be used as a precursor to out loud empathy, but it can also be used simply as a way to connect with the other person through the needs you imagine they might have been meeting.

In doing silent empathy, you keep your focus on what needs the other person might be trying to meet, without going into analyses of their behavior. It is not as important to be right as it is to be aware that the other person is acting to meet their needs just as you are, and to connect with those needs instead of with your judgment about people's strategies for meeting their needs. Even though this process happens without the other person's awareness of it, if you practice keeping your focus on needs, you might notice that your own energy shifts. You will be a different person, and hence will act and speak out of this shifted sense of self. Others will respond to this shift regardless of whether your internal guesses as to their needs are correct.

Practice Pause

Think back to your most recent interaction with someone, however brief. What need might that person have been trying to meet with their words or actions?

Silent empathy can be done regarding any interaction with another person, while you are having the conversation or afterward. While you are learning, we suggest practicing with any actions or words you hear from others, whether directed at you or not, and whether you find them enjoyable or triggering. In doing so, you will gain skill and facility in staying connected with needs and in guessing what needs others might be seeking to meet by their actions. Silent empathy can also be used at work during meetings, in anticipation of a meeting, or in mourning or celebrating after a meeting as part of the learning process. (See Example 4 on facing page.)

For example, when I am in a meeting, I stay with silent empathy to the extent I am able to. When I get stimulated by something I or someone else says or does, then I go back to self-empathy, because I'm no longer connected with other people's needs. Once I've reconnected to myself sufficiently, I'm able to listen for what the person is really saying, what I imagine their reason is for saying it, and what the need is that they're seeking to meet. What I like about switching back and forth this way, between silent empathy and self-empathy, is that even if I don't say anything directly using NVC—Observations, Feeling, Needs, Requests, either in the form of empathy or expression—I am a different person than if I'm thinking judgmental thoughts. I'm coming out of a different energy. A person will react to me differently because of my body language, the words I use and how I use them, the pacing, pressure, and energy that's in my voice. My entire demeanor will be different as a result of doing these practices of self-empathy and silent empathy in the moment.

In summary, thus far we suggest using NVC in your workplace through awareness of how you are blocking connection, and through using self-empathy and silent empathy whenever possible. As you begin to practice these skills, you will probably find yourself reviewing situations, focusing on what else you might have done, and solidifying your intention to do things differently next time. If so, then you are now in the learning cycle, which we will look at in more depth in the next chapter.

Example 4

You have another meeting with your team, two weeks later. You realize going into the meeting that you have preconceived ideas of how the meeting will go, based on your experience meeting with these folks for the last six

months. You don't like the feelings, thoughts, and
actions that result from these judgments. This time,
you decide to try using your silent empathy practice
to change your experience during the meeting. You
pay attention carefully for when you are triggered by
Harold or someone else. As soon as you notice it, you
use self-empathy in the moment (alternately paying
attention to the meeting) to reconnect with your needs.
You might write on your notepad what was said or done
that triggered you, how you feel about it, and what need
of yours is not met. Having reconnected with yourself,
you switch to silent empathy—to guessing what might be
stimulating the other person, what they might be feeling,
and what need they are seeking to meet. During the rest
of the meeting, you find yourself shifting to self-empathy
and silent empathy whenever you realize you've been
triggered.

Chapter 3

The Learning Cycle:
Celebrating Progress, Mourning Mistakes

Celebration and mourning are processes we can use to shift us out of a blaming and punishing mentality. These practices help us see and step out of the game of looking for who is at fault—you or someone else—for what is not right about a situation.

We all play this game, every waking moment; it is embedded in our language. "He's not at fault." "She didn't have any other alternative." "So what else could they have done?" "I had to do it." The feelings associated with blaming and punishing are anger, depression, shame, and guilt. These feelings tend to be stimulated by what we are thinking and telling ourselves. I find it very difficult to learn how to meet my needs when I am assessing blame, avoiding punishment, and alternately feeling angry, depressed, ashamed, or guilty. My guess is other people do too.

We can use celebration and mourning to shift into learning. I suggest you try the celebration and mourning practices in the learning cycle discussed below with interactions with coworkers, whether you enjoyed the interaction or not. These are practices you do without the coworker being present. You can do this entirely in your head, or out loud with the support of a friend. You can start as soon as you become aware that you did or did not enjoy an interaction, or you can start later, whenever you feel more at ease doing so.

Celebrating and Mourning in NVC

If you enjoyed an interaction with a coworker, then you will be celebrating the needs met. Think about what specific observations you can make about the interaction, how you feel now recalling the situation, and what needs of yours those feelings arise out of. (This is a present tense activity and not an inquiry into your feelings and needs at the time of the original event.) As you recall the part of the interaction that you are focusing on for celebration or mourning, ask yourself, "How do I feel and which of my needs are being met as I am feeling this feeling?" Thus celebration is in part a method of learning how you experience your needs being met in the moment when reflecting upon an instance in the past. Moreover, by inference, you are also learning how your needs might be met in similar situations in the future. Celebration connects needs being met. This is the heart of gratitude—feeling grateful for what you and others have done to create the world more to your liking. The process leads you to active awareness of what meets your needs and focuses your mind on seeking to create more of the same.

Similarly, the process of mourning also leads to learning, except that it focuses on aspects of our experience where our needs were not met. For example, perhaps at work I had an encounter at the metaphorical water cooler, experiencing a situation where others were gossiping. I was uncomfortable with what was going on, yet I was not clear in myself what it was I didn't like about it. I was also unhappy with the fact that I stayed silent, yet I couldn't think of anything to say. This is where the learning process of mourning becomes helpful. I connect, preferably immediately, or as soon after as I can, with what I feel and the need that is not met as I recall the event. This connection is a way of mourning that I did not act as I would have liked. When I connect with the need that was not met, I know I've connected with the need I want to be met, and my mind then looks for strategies to meet it. I can then consciously role-play, in my imagination or with a learning companion, how I would have liked to communicate. (See Example 5 on facing page.)

Example 5

During an interaction with your coworker Karen, she says: "How come we haven't seen your part of the project yet? You said you'd have it done by now." Defensively, you say, "Well, I haven't seen your or Harold's part of the project either; how come you're bugging me?" The conversation ends with Karen saying, "Yeah, Harold and I are done; we're just waiting for you."

You immediately realize how terrible you feel, so you decide to go for a walk so you can use the learning cycle. You say to yourself: "When I think about what Karen said, I feel irritated because I need understanding and consideration about why I'm not complete with my work on the project. When I think about what I said, I feel disappointed because my needs for consideration and kindness were not met."

You notice the sadness that arises realizing those needs were not met. You imagine what your experience would be like if those needs were being met, and find your heart opening and your energy lightening. Then you consider how you might have acted. "I would have liked to have said: 'I'm not ready to give it to you because I've been focusing on this other project for Magna, and I'm regretting that I underestimated how much time it was going to take for me to complete this project. I estimate I will be able to get my part to you by the end of the week; will that work for you?'"

After having gone through this process, you feel compassion for both yourself and Karen.

Let's look at another example to see how mourning practice might proceed. A coworker, we'll call him Adrian, walked into the room you were in and said hello to you, and you didn't respond. Later, you realize that you are judging yourself for not responding. You think, "Wow, I was really rude to Adrian." Realizing that this is an opportunity to engage with the learning cycle instead of staying stuck in a judgment, you might go through a process such as the following:

First, you begin with self-empathy: "When I tell myself, 'I'm rude,' I feel lousy because I need self-care." In this statement, you focus on the current thought in your head ("I am rude") and identify the need not met by it. Then, you might look at the need not met in the events that stimulated that thought: "When I remember not responding to Adrian this morning after he said hello, I feel sad because my need for consideration is not met." Another step is recognizing that you were meeting some needs with the action you chose (to not say hello). You might then say to yourself, "When I remember the needs for focus and attention I was meeting at the time, I feel reassured because my need for understanding is being met."

Self-empathy often creates the inner sense of well-being that allows you to shift to empathy for the other person: "When I remember the look on Adrian's face when I did not respond to his hello, I feel tender and wonder if he is feeling hurt and needing consideration." Connecting with your own needs and your guess as to Adrian's needs then leads to thinking of strategies to follow up from this interaction. If you are feeling confident enough to try some out loud skills, you might want to ask Adrian the next time you see him, "Would you be willing to speak with me for a couple of minutes about the other day when you said hello to me and I did not respond?" Assuming he says yes, there are a couple of options you might choose: either to practice out loud empathy or to express your honesty. If you choose empathy, you might say, "When you remember that, are you feeling hurt because you would like consideration for your feelings?" If you choose expression, you could say: "When I remember my focus yesterday that led me to not respond, I feel sad because I would like consideration. How do you feel when you hear me say that?"

Depending on how this interaction goes, you can then enter back into the learning cycle—celebrating or mourning the needs met or not met in this new interaction. In Chapter 6, we will discuss in more depth the learning cycle as it relates in particular to preparing for and having difficult conversations in the workplace. (See Example 6 below.)

Example 6

Later that day, you run into Karen in the hallway, and, with your heart pounding, manage to say something very close to what you had practiced on your walk. When you ask Karen if it will work to get your part of the project to her by the end of the week, she says: "Yes, that will be fine. And let me know if there's anything I can do to help." You decide to use the learning cycle again, and think to yourself: "When I recall what Karen said, I feel relieved because my needs for understanding and support are met, and I also feel happy that I spoke to her again about it, as it helped me feel some mastery and hope. I wonder if her response came from her desire to contribute." In holding all of these needs, you feel a certain satisfaction and appreciation for your willingness to use this situation as a learning. To further the learning opportunity, you ask yourself, "What can I learn from this sequence of events?" One thing you conclude is that the next time there is a similar situation, you might feel more confident to engage Karen in the moment instead of doing an off-line learning process before reengaging with her.

Through silent practice, we learn the skills that will help us trust that we can speak up when necessary and also respond in a way we would like to, whatever reactions our speaking up engenders. It often takes a number of learning cycles to develop the facility to respond from our authentic needs in situations that trigger us. For example, I have used this learning process when some members of my extended family told jokes about race and sex that I found painful to listen to. This is a situation many people encounter in the workplace as well (Chapter 6 also discusses humor in the workplace). In using the mourning process after these experiences, I began to gain confidence that I might be able to respond in ways that would be congruent with my values and, at the same time, would continue my relationship with the person telling the joke. I had to repeat the mourning process many times, however, in order to have the presence to reconnect with myself and adapt the language I had practiced in role-play to the situation. Particularly when we are stimulated in ways that remind us of how we were hurt when we were young, it may take us many mourning cycles of reconnection with ourselves to be willing to speak up. Similarly, it may take a while to develop your trust in yourself that you will respond to the other person's reactions the way you would like.

Putting the Learning Cycle Into Daily Practice

Besides taking a short amount of time after a situation to engage in the mourning or celebration learning cycle, we suggest incorporating it as part of a daily practice. For me, this works best in the morning, reviewing the day before; it could also be done in the evening, reviewing the current day.

I simply review the day before, and remember a situation that did or did not unfold as I would have liked. I practice the distinctions of Nonviolent Communication by first stating what happened in observation language. Then, staying in the present tense, I identify my feelings now, as I recall that incident, and the need that is or is not met in this moment when I think about what happened. Finally, I think about what, if any, requests I might formulate about this situation. Depending on the day, I might make sure my practice includes at least one situation for mourning and one for celebration.

Practice Pause

Choose one recent situation where you would like to have acted differently. Take a moment to mourn, and consider how you would like to have acted.

The four main benefits of a daily mourning and celebration practice are that it serves as a reminder to use NVC, enhances your abilities with the four basic distinctions, shifts you out of blame and into learning, and provides a daily dose of empathy and gratitude. Let's discuss each one of these benefits, and in doing so, unpack this practice further.

In the beginning of learning to incorporate a new skill, it is crucial to find ways to remind ourselves that it is an option. When we get caught up in our day-to-day lives, it is easy to forget that we wanted to incorporate NVC. A commitment to a daily practice can remind us that these skills are available and that we are interested in trying them out. It can be helpful to have another person involved for accountability and extra support, so if you can find someone to have a daily mourning and celebration phone call with, that's an extra bonus. Basically, this practice reconnects us on an ongoing basis with our intention to use NVC.

The daily mourning and celebration practice also helps the NVC distinctions become more ingrained and easier to make. The first thing I do, once I've remembered a situation I want to mourn or celebrate, is to state it in observation language, which can be a learning in and of itself. I must exercise the mental muscle of seeing what is a judgment and what is an observation. Seeing that distinction and making the conversion from judgment to observation each day allows me to do it in my daily life more easily. It becomes almost automatic. My feelings and needs vocabulary increases as well. I have often found myself identifying a feeling that I cannot name, or finding the names I do come up with do not quite name it. I then go looking for the name of it, using one of the long lists available in Marshall Rosenberg's books, in handouts from trainers, or online from CNVC (see Appendix B for a Feelings list). Identifying the feeling increases the likelihood that I'll remember that name next time and associate it with that feeling. This goes for needs as well; identifying the needs met and not met helps me identify the patterns of needs that I am commonly in touch with (see Appendix D for a Needs list). Naming them increases familiarity and eventually creates proficiency in identifying them in the moment.

For me, the fundamental benefit of my daily practice has been the shift out of the blame and punishment paradigm and into the learning paradigm. If I'm not connected with myself, and I'm finding the memory of something that happened the day before painful, I am typically in a blame and punishment paradigm. That means I'm blaming either somebody else or myself for what was or was not done. This paradigm is dominant in our culture, and it stems from a focus on what we do not like. In this paradigm, we see what we don't like, name it, and criticize it. For example, I don't like someone's rude behavior toward me, and I either say something to them out loud or hold it in my head. The problem with this way of approaching the situation is that the mind fixates on the judgment—"this person is rude"—and nothing transforms. I have found that it does not work for me simply to tell myself not to blame myself or another person. If, however, I use the mourning process and state an observation—"this person is acting in a way I don't enjoy, that doesn't meet my need for respect"—now I am in touch with the longing for the need for respect to be met. Now, my mind has shifted to something that it can transform; it is looking for how it can get the need for respect met. That may be by saying something, or it may be by connecting with myself to the extent that I don't interpret what the other person says in the same way. Either way, the thought is transformed, and therefore so are the behaviors stemming from it. With practice and over time, the blame paradigm itself slowly shifts and is replaced by the learning paradigm.

The final benefit of a daily mourning and celebration practice is that it feels good. Checking in with feelings and needs meets our need for empathy. I often find that for me, it results in feeling a kind of sweet sadness, a connection with myself and compassion for myself and others. If the incident I practiced with that day involved a situation with someone else, my practice often leads to a desire to express appreciation to that person; I have often recontacted the person and taken the opportunity to practice expressing appreciation. Seeing the gift of appreciation received, and receiving back the gift of it having been received, is very sweet, and I believe also has health benefits for both parties.

Creating a mourning and celebration practice for yourself, through both daily practice and in-the-moment responses to situations that arise, can prove to be an important factor in your ability to quickly integrate the skills of NVC into your life. It can also be a good antidote to burnout. Though you may not be ready yet to incorporate a mourning and celebration practice with your coworkers, I believe the ability for work groups to celebrate and mourn on a regular basis, even for just a few minutes, provides nourishment that forestalls burnout. I have incorporated it into my work life and interactions with my work colleagues; we have an identified period of time to celebrate and mourn. If you are not comfortable discussing these concepts with your colleagues, you might be able to introduce it more subtly, focusing on celebration. When something happens, even if it seems small, take a moment publicly to acknowledge and celebrate that occurrence. If you do this often enough, you might find colleagues copying your example, without your having formally introduced any NVC.

Practice Pause

Think of something that happened at work recently, however small, that you liked. How might you be able to celebrate it with your coworkers?

Chapter 4

Practice:
Building Confidence and Competence

Incorporating new communication skills takes practice. We frequently forget this. All too often, we act as if we should be able to immediately incorporate a new skill without time or effort. We have this kind of magical thinking where we believe that once we have understood something conceptually, we will be able to do it; however, there is a difference between understanding something and doing it. We usually face a learning curve before we become comfortable with a new way of doing something, and NVC is no exception. It may be helpful to remember this when in the workplace—where you already have a history and habitual way of behaving. The key to moving through the learning curve and gaining competence is practice. In this section, we will discuss what to practice, when, and with whom, all with an eye toward gaining fluency in silent practices—and eventually out loud practices—in your workplace.

Practicing Silent Skills

A major benefit to the self-empathy and silent empathy skills discussed in Chapter 2 is that they can be practiced anytime and anywhere. Both are ideal to practice in your car on the way to work (driving often provides multiple triggers, and thus multiple opportunities to reconnect to your needs and guess the needs of other drivers), or standing in line at the grocery store, or on hold waiting for a client or customer service representative. Self-empathy can also be used in all those small moments that usually pass by unused, such as walking from your office to the copy machine or after dialing the phone. The more practice you get, the more easily and quickly you will be able to identify and connect with your needs in each moment, including moments when you are triggered.

Practice Pause

Think of five things you do multiple times a day where you could remind yourself to engage in silent practice.

Another ideal opportunity to practice is when watching TV, reading newspapers or magazines, or listening to political talk shows. I regularly listen to political talk radio, both left and right, until I get triggered; then I turn it off and do self-empathy. There have been times driving my car that I have had to pull off the road when listening to someone I profoundly disagreed with. Through my self-empathy and silent empathy practice, I connected so deeply with what I was able to guess were the needs in what commentators were saying that I started to tear up. Of course, this doesn't happen very often; I listen every chance I get to those I disagree with, and it often does not take long before I am triggered.

Practicing Out Loud Skills

It is also helpful to practice out loud with other people, to get the immediate feedback of others' reactions and to practice noticing your reaction to their response. Who you choose to practice with, however, can make all the difference between your continuing to practice and gain confidence in these skills, or giving up before you have really given it a chance.

I think of relationships as existing in three concentric circles. The innermost circle consists of your intimate relationships—those people with whom you communicate frequently. This inner circle differs from person to person. It may include intimate partners, family members, and even people you are close to in your work. These people will definitely notice if you suddenly start communicating differently; they are the most familiar with you. The outermost circle consists of people you interact with who don't know you—you have had no past communication with them, and you aren't necessarily very likely to stay in contact with them. These are people such as salespeople, taxi drivers, and telephone customer support people that you interact with in the course of daily life. The middle circle includes people with whom you have enough contact that they will know if you start communicating differently, but who are not intimates. For many people, the middle circle is likely to include people in their workplace.

The two main groups of people I suggest you practice out loud with are your innermost and outermost circles, with an important distinction between how you approach them. As you begin your out loud practice, I suggest you continue to practice silently with those in your middle circle.

The easiest group to practice out loud with is the outermost circle. If you practice self-expression and empathy with people you don't know, they have no prior expectation about how you communicate. They may think it odd, but they are much less likely to react than are people who know your typical communication patterns. In fact, I've never had someone in an outermost-circle context tell me that I'm talking weird, or react to what I'm saying; they simply have no experience of me otherwise. Examples of who to practice with in this category might be people you meet in passing, such as service people, waitstaff, or clerks. These people not only don't know you, but you are unlikely to meet them again, much less form a continuing relationship. If you feel comfortable doing so, you could also practice with new people you meet in your workplace or in social circles, people with whom you may form continuing relationships in the future.

To practice with the innermost circle, those people who will notice that you are doing something different, I have found it is better to get their buy-in. It is not likely to go over well if you practice with them without their agreement to participate in that practice. In the workplace, the innermost circle would be the people with whom you feel the safest, and with whom you feel comfortable developing a new way of communicating. If you want to practice with your innermost circle at work or at home, let them know that you would like to practice this skill and what it is (if they do not already know), and form agreements with them around practice.

Making Agreements to Practice NVC

One example of this type of agreement would be for you to say to one of your innermost circle: "I am interested in something called Nonviolent Communication, and I'm going to start trying to use it more, so I'm going to be saying some things in ways that are a little different from before. If at any time you feel uncomfortable or you don't like what I'm saying, I'd really like to hear it right away, and for us to deal with it." Then, end on a request: "Are you willing to tell me when you don't like the way I'm talking with you?" If they agree, then work from that agreement. This agreement encourages them to bring it up if they do feel uncomfortable, and reduces the anxiety they might have about expressing their discomfort.

From your perspective, since you have not only agreed but have actually requested they bring any discomfort up, this agreement tends to reduce the typical reaction of interpreting their comments as criticism and being resistant to hearing what they have to say.

This kind of agreement also tends to result in people more readily telling you what they like about how you are learning to communicate, even though that aspect of feedback is not explicitly addressed in the agreement.

Practice Pause

Whom in your inner circle might you make a practice agreement with? Practice how you might phrase your request.

Pitfalls of Practicing Without Agreements

I stress making these types of agreements with those close to you because in my own experience I have encountered the pitfalls of practicing with people in my innermost circle without these agreements. I have found lack of agreement creates difficulties both with family and with workplace relationships. Once, when I was first learning about NVC and trying to incorporate it into my life, I was driving with my wife and adolescent daughter. At some point, I asked my daughter to tell me her feelings about something, and she said: "I have no feelings, needs, or requests. Let's move on."

In other conversations with her and her two brothers during this period, my interpretation was that they were getting an inconsistent message about compassion from me. I was using NVC as a strategy to help me remember and be present, but I was not as consistent as I would have liked. They were therefore often getting the "old Ike"—acting out of judgment and demand—even when using the form of this new approach. My guess is that their needs for genuineness, trust, and predictability were not getting met.

What to do in that moment, however, when someone close to you reacts? When my daughter said, "I have no feelings, needs, or requests, let's move on," my reaction was to feel confused and uncomfortable. Self-empathy was therefore the first thing I needed to do. I longed for connection with my daughter, and wanted to be seen for my intention and caring. After connecting with my own needs, I could guess what was going on for her silently, then maybe ultimately say something out loud. Silently, I might guess that she had a need for genuineness and trust—trust that there would be consistency from me in this demand-versus-request continuum.

An empathic response to her in that situation (which I did not do), might have been, "Are you feeling irritated because you want predictability in the way I react to you, or you want a kind of genuineness?" My guess is that stated in that language, she might have been stimulated even further. So I might translate it into something I could imagine she would hear more easily, but still trying to focus on her needs. An example of that might be, "Are you doubting that you are going to be heard the way you would like if I speak like this?" or "Do you want it to be easier to talk with us?" If I wanted to take my wife and myself out of the need, I might say something like, "Do you want it to be easier to communicate?" or "Do you want communicating to be easier?"

Another alternative would be to express my reaction. For example, I might say: "When I hear you say 'I have no feelings, needs, or requests, let's move on,' I feel frustrated because I want to figure out some way of being able to talk with you and get across how much I care and want to support you. Would you be willing to tell me how you feel hearing what I just said?" Or I might say a similar thing, but my request might be, "Would you be willing to spend five minutes with me right now figuring out how we can talk with each other so that we can hear what each of us wants the other to hear?"

I experienced similar reactions from my work colleagues when I was first incorporating NVC into my life. At that time, I was a partner in a law firm I had cofounded, and I had initially been interested in NVC as a means of improving what I called the *billiard-shot communication* in our firm. This was my attempt to describe situations when two people get into a conflict and then for days, or weeks, will not talk or interact unless absolutely necessary. I am confident that you have experienced something similar. The way this happened in our office is that after the initial conflict, the participants would not talk with each other, though they did talk to others in the office about the situation. It seemed to me that they were seeking to get others to collude with them as to their view of the person they were distressed with. I called this billiard-shot communication because they would ricochet their communication back to the "other" through the rest of us.

As a manager I tried two strategies. First was denial. This was my default approach. I avoided the conflict and hoped it would go away. This response made a lot of sense given my dismal success at seeking to intervene to change this dynamic.

However, at times I would realize the situation was so impacting our capacity to represent our clients to my standards that I brought the parties together and sought to foster a conversation. The times I tried this, I only made matters worse. The combination of my lack of skills, my attempt to force reconciliation, and my role as co-owner and manager worked together to add fuel to the fire of conflict they were already stoking. So now they would be pissed off at me as well as each other. In retrospect, I now guess that they were further distressed by not being heard by me as they would have liked. So in addition to the hurt they were carrying from the conflict with each other, they were now additionally hurt by not getting their need to be heard in this second forum. Added to that was all the uncertainty that was likely stimulated in them by concerns about how my reaction might affect needs that were tied to their employment.

One of the things I regret about this early period of incorporating NVC into my life, while I was still practicing law, was that I did not make the kinds of practice agreements I am talking about here with the people with whom I worked. About the time I withdrew from the practice of law, I began to make practice agreements with my colleagues. For example, I asked people I worked with to bring to my attention when I used a judgment in place of an observation. During this period, I found it much easier to have a person with whom I had such an agreement bring this to my attention. If someone else volunteered this "helpful" bit of support, someone I had not chosen to involve in my education, I would typically react out of my need for respect for my autonomy. Now, in situations when a person says something like, "Isn't that a judgment you just used?" I am more inclined to hear this as being about their need for understanding rather than as a critique of my awareness.

Similarly, I have asked for help in learning how to make requests that are doable, present tense, and in action language. This has been an ongoing learning process for me. On innumerable occasions, I have engaged my work colleagues to help me formulate requests that might meet my needs, and that at the same time would be received by them as a doable request. Not infrequently on these occasions, my starting point was an expression of my dream of what the state of affairs would be after my colleagues had done what I had asked them to do. I wanted my dream to come about without actually asking them to do what it would take. I was in effect asking them to figure out what they might do to fulfill my dream, and then to do it. Another way to look at it is that I did not do the work of figuring out what it was that I wanted them to do. Moreover, at times I was not willing to risk revealing what I really wanted them to do. Instead, I would state my dream in hopes my needs would be satisfied. As a result of seeing myself and others do this time and again, I have developed the following ironic aphorism: "In most situations, I will increase the likelihood of getting what I want if I ask for it."

What do I mean by asking for my dream to be fulfilled instead of making a request? Telling a person that I need help and saying, "Will you help me?" is a simple example of a dream rather than a request. Of course, if colleagues have enough prior experience with each other in similar situations, they might be confident that they know what "help" would look like. However, as is often the case, even if I am clear I need help, and I am willing to ask for it, I may have difficulty articulating what I would like someone to do that they have the capacity to do (doable); what I would like them to do now, in the moment (present tense); what I would like them to do, as opposed to what I would like them to stop doing (action language); and finally, what I am able to ask for that is truly a request, and not a demand. (See Chapter 5 for examples of making clear requests in the workplace.)

Ways to Practice With NVC Agreements

Perhaps you have buy-in from those close to you: they are ready for a change in how you communicate with them and have readily agreed to be part of your practice, or, if you are very lucky, they have also taken NVC workshops and are simultaneously working on incorporating it into their lives. There are specific agreements that you can make with people to help support you in your learning, besides the generic agreement to be part of the process. The two types of agreements I'll discuss and give examples of below are agreements reflecting the distinctions of NVC, and accountability agreements.

Awareness Agreements

You recall each of the four communication parts has a distinction that accompanies it—Observations versus judgments, Feelings versus evaluations masquerading as feelings, Needs versus strategies, and Requests versus demands. There are agreements you can make with people in your life to keep clarifying and refining your understanding of any one of these distinctions. You might have an agreement with someone you trust to point out to you when you use judgments. This helps you develop awareness of how frequently you use judgmental language and prompts you to identify the observations. In another example, I have had a series of agreements with work colleagues concerning the distinction between a request and a demand. The agreement comes out of a shared understanding of the distinction and an assurance that we only want each other to respond to requests. If the receiver of the request has any interpretation that it might be a demand, then we don't want that person to agree to it. In other words, if either of us is agreeing in order to avoid punishment, criticism, or some future attempt to induce shame or guilt, then we are interpreting it as a demand, and would not agree to it.

I have explicitly had this very agreement with people who act in an administrative support role for me. Even with a person who has agreed to do certain categories of tasks for me, it is important to me that I request they do this next task, and not demand or expect it. I believe this more accurately reflects the reality of the workplace. In fact, even though the other person may acquiesce this time, unless they are willing to do what I ask, there will be consequences in due course. And these consequences might include quitting, doing the task without the kind of attention to quality that I would like, or just in general negatively affecting the rapport I would like to enjoy with the people I work with. On the occasions when a coworker has not been willing to do what I ask, I have found that if I am willing to be curious and to listen, there is something valuable for me to learn from their no.

There does not have to be this shared understanding on both sides, however. As long as one person is clear about the distinction, and the liabilities of having those close to them give in to demands, the agreement can still be made. In this case, the request might sound something like this: "I'm trying this new thing called NVC that's affecting the way I interact. I will be making requests of you, but if at any time you hear it as a demand, I'd like you to tell me. That is, if at any time you have any sense that if you don't do what I ask, then I'll attempt to punish you or induce shame or guilt, I'd like you to tell me at that time. Are you willing to do that?"

This type of agreement plays out in the moment as follows: Say that I have made a request to a coworker, and after several exchanges about it, they suddenly shift or agree to do what is being asked. At this point, I might check in and say something like "I just want to check whether you are shifting or giving in, because I don't want to pay the price of you giving in. Are you hearing this as a demand in any way?" The other person then has the opportunity to reflect and clarify their own sense of the shift, and whether they are interpreting the request as a demand. It is also a chance for me to reflect (especially if I am not crystal clear yet on this distinction) on whether I truly am making a request, or whether there is any hint of demand hidden within: any sense that it would not be OK for the request to be turned down.

Accountability Agreements

The other type of agreements we can make to support our learning I call accountability agreements. These agreements are based on our knowledge that while we are attempting to incorporate a new set of values and skills into our lives, the reality is that we will likely be triggered in heated moments to react out of our habitual patterns. We make *accountability agreements* with people close to us to empower them, if they see us acting in a way they interpret as out of alignment with how we have stated we want to act, to call us on it in a previously agreed-upon way.

I regularly now make accountability agreements with the people I work with. Yet I want to give you another example of an agreement with my daughter because it has so much meaning for me and because it conveys the same structure and purpose as the agreements I use now with my colleagues.

I made this accountability agreement with my daughter when she was about fifteen. At the time, I was trying to learn how to interact in a way where I did not seek to use power over people to get my way. I had noticed this tendency throughout my life, but it was particularly painful to see when I did it with my wife and children. I found that I would start out with the intention not to use power over, but then I would get triggered and lose track of my intention. I would even lose track that I had lost track, and then I would start to use my size, presence, and years of experience as a trial lawyer to try to force people into doing what I wanted.

I made an agreement with my daughter that if she saw me acting in a way that she guessed was me attempting to use power over another person, she would ask me this question: "Dad, is this what you want to do with your life?" When I discussed making this agreement with her, we came up with this question together; it is important that the specific question be agreed upon beforehand, so it can act as a hook to pull you back to your intention in the moment.

This agreement played out one night at the dinner table. I got into an exchange with one of my sons, who was seventeen at the time. I don't remember the specific topic, but he was acting out of his needs for autonomy and respect: he had a viewpoint and wanted to be heard. I was triggered and wanted to have my way, and it turned into the typical father-son challenge. I was completely lost in it. My daughter had to interrupt me to get my attention, then she asked me, "Dad, is this what you want to do with your life?"

I remembered the agreement, but I was irritated by her question. Because I had asked her to do it, I didn't direct my irritation at her, but I bristled, then turned back to my exchanges with my son. She interrupted me again, "Dad, is this what you want to do with your life?" Again, I bristled, and then went back to going at it with my son, but I'd shifted a little bit. She interrupted me a third time. That one got to me, and I was flummoxed and stuck.

I turned to my son and I said: "I'm not doing what I want to be doing. I don't know how to do it right now, and so I'm going to leave, because I can't be with you the way I'd like to be. I'll be back, but I need some time." I went upstairs and took the time I needed, and then I reengaged later, after the dinner was over. That's an example of empowering someone in the world around you to support you in staying in alignment with or returning to your values.

The following is an example of using accountability agreements in a workplace environment. For many years, my workplace included courtrooms. Once I was in the early part of a trial where I was counsel for a party in the lawsuit. My client, the plaintiff, we'll call Joe Brown. I had become used to calling him by his first name in the course of working with him to prepare the lawsuit. At one of the first breaks in trial, after the jury had left the courtroom, the judge directed that I not use my client's first name when referring to him during my examination of witnesses, as it was too familiar and biased the jury toward my case; the defense lawyer, out of a sense of court decorum, was constrained to address him as Mr. Brown. I agreed to do the same, then continued with my examination of witnesses, only to again be admonished by the judge, at the next break, to refer to Joe as plaintiff or Mr. Brown. I had no awareness of calling him by his first name, and had every intention of complying with the judge's order. Yet this continued happening until the judge told me (again outside the presence of the jury) that I would be held in contempt of court if I did not stop using Joe's first name.

At this point I was very distressed, as I did not know what to do to avoid being held in contempt. I told the judge that I was unaware of when I was calling my client by his first name, and I asked if he (the judge) would be willing to tell me the next time I did so. He said he would not do that in front of the jury, as that might prejudice my client's case. I then turned to my client and asked him if the next time he heard me call him Joe, he would clear his throat. He agreed. Soon after the jury returned and we began again, I heard Joe clear his throat as I was posing a question, and I realized immediately and made the correction. This only had to happen a couple of times before I was able to catch myself and make the correction before speaking his name. Having the presence of mind to request help and make an agreement around an unconscious behavior helped me become aware of that behavior very quickly, as well as saved me from being held in contempt of court!

In a situation such as this, we may have enough anxiety that we will not immediately be able to come up with the request we would like to make. We may need a time-out.

Practice Pause

Consider what type of agreement—awareness or accountability—might help you most in your practice. Whom might you ask to assist you with this agreement?

Taking the Time You Need

As the above stories exemplify, an important part of practice is to realize that the learning curve initially may be steep, and in some cases you may not respond as you would like or even be able to stay with your intention. In these cases, taking a time-out may be appropriate. Sometimes, in the workplace, the best we are able to do may be to remove ourselves from the situation in order to give ourselves empathy and reconnect with our needs. Then we are more likely to be able to reengage in the way we would like. (See Example 7 on facing page.)

You can anticipate these situations by practicing how to articulate a time-out. There are elements of a time-out that I like to hear if someone takes a time-out from me. I like to hear the person say that it is about themselves, that they're not able to do what they would like to do in the situation, that they are going to take some time but do intend to come back (if they do), and that they're taking the time-out so they can have the space they need in order to be and act the way they would like to. It might sound something like this: "Excuse me, I need to take a break. I'm stimulated; I'm not able to be with you the way I'd like, and when I'm able to reengage with some hope of being able to do it the way I would like, I'll come back." Notice that the focus is on the speaker and what the speaker is able to do and not do. There is no judgment of the other person suggested as the cause of the time-out. You might even want to say, "This is not about you; it is about me and what's going on inside of me."

Of course, a time-out may also sound like this: "Excuse me, I'm going to the bathroom." I've used this in legal mediations that I do as a result of being on the federal court panel of mediators. Sometimes you can include a little more connection, but if you are highly triggered, it may be best to simply excuse yourself.

Without practice, it is unlikely that your intention to connect and communicate with others will ever be realized. It helps to find ways to remind ourselves to practice, which can include posting notes in places we will see them, engaging those in our lives to help us, and creating specific times to practice, as we discussed earlier with the mourning and celebration daily practice. With these reminders firmly in place and a commitment to practicing every chance you get, whether silently or out loud, your intention will undoubtedly manifest and positively affect your life in ways you may not now be able to envision.

Example 7

You and Harold get into a heated exchange concerning the best way to proceed on a new project. As you feel your anger growing and hear your voice rising, you realize that you are not acting as you would like and will not be able to without taking some time to reconnect with your needs. You take a breath and say to Harold: "OK, I'm not able to see this clearly right now or interact with you the way I would like, and I need to take some time to think it over. I'd like to come back after lunch to talk to you about this." Harold, still in the heat of the moment, continues to talk. You interrupt him, saying: "Excuse me, Harold, I need to take a break now. I'm not able to talk to you about this in a way that I feel comfortable about, so I'm going to take some time, and I will get back to you after lunch." Then you walk away to find a quiet place to do self-empathy.

Practice Pause

Create a "practice plan" that includes a specific daily practice, ideas for reminding yourself to practice during the day, and people you will enlist to support you.

Chapter 5

Powerful Requests:
Asking for What You Want

In the workplace, and in life in general, it often seems like the dissatisfaction and frustration people experience from not getting their needs met stems from the fact that they often don't ask for what they want in an effective way. Some people fear the vulnerability they think they will experience if they ask for what they really want. Also, in this culture we generally do not get a lot of training regarding how to make requests.

Recognizing Typical Patterns in Unclear Requests

In practicing requests in my own life, I have noticed two things that I consistently do that get in the way of making clear requests: self-editing and thinking I've asked for something when I have not.

Self-editing refers to conversations in our head, when we are thinking about what we want, that run something like this: "Well, I really want him to let me know ahead of time when he is going to spring a completely new project on me so I can prepare for it. But he has always done this and he won't change, and even if he does, I still will have to fit it in to everything else I'm already doing, so why bother asking for it?" I think my needs are not going to get met, and I think asking might undermine our relationship, so I won't even ask. I have experienced this form of self-editing, and I imagine others have also. When I notice I'm self-editing, I begin to realize that I'm operating out of some beliefs—about the other person or the situation, or perhaps even myself. With this awareness, I can then look at those beliefs, find the need behind them, and inquire into whether I want to test them by, perhaps, making a request.

Another pattern I notice is how I think I am asking for something, but when I analyze what I've said, I haven't asked for anything after all. For example, perhaps I tell someone a dream of mine, something I really want to happen in my life. My relating this dream may be leading up to a request—perhaps I want this person to hear my dream; perhaps I want a certain kind of response from them. This person might interpret a request and respond, and I might be satisfied; nevertheless, there have been times enough when if I don't state the request, I do not get back what I want. In these cases, I notice a tendency to blame the other person for not giving me what I thought I had asked for, even though looking closely at the interaction, I might notice that I had never stated a clear request. Between couples this often shows up in the statement "Well, you know what I meant," a response I have heard from my wife. In my own practice, I don't want to rely upon the other person having to guess what I meant, as in my experience, that often leads to not getting my needs met.

Getting Clear on Making Clear Requests

The process of formulating a request helps me clarify my needs. I find that if I'm not clear about my needs when I actually put words to the request, it doesn't work. To make a request presupposes that I have done my work to be clear about what need I want this request to meet. I once heard a teacher say that if one person becomes clear, it provides the opportunity for those around them to become clear. So the clearer I get, the clearer my request gets, and the clearer the other person can be about their own response to it.

Getting clear also helps move me out of complaining and feeling hopeless and powerless. I think that's because of the way the mind works. If you give the human mind the need, or that which you would like to create in the world, the mind will start scanning the horizon, metaphorically, looking for strategies to meet the need. For example, say I'm connecting with my longing for a certain quality of contribution in my life; I've realized that need and mourned that I'm not getting it met in the way that I would like. My consciousness may shift then to going about my life, but there's a part of my mind that seems to continue to process and look for opportunities to meet the need for contribution. Thus, the clarity about what needs are not being met, gained through the mourning process and connecting with what needs you want to be met, seems to have the power to get us to look for strategies to meet the need rather than obsess about instances when the need has not been met.

Knowing before you start speaking what need you're trying to get met and what your request is has a couple of benefits: it fulfills your need for empathy and reduces the number of words you use. The process of getting clear about your needs is the process of self-empathy, and we've already noted (and perhaps by now you have experienced) how your energy shifts when your need for empathy has been met. When you are clear about your request, you usually find you can state it in a few words. When you reduce the number of words and speak from the shifted energy of empathic connection with yourself, you increase the likelihood that your request will be heard as you intend. That is, the needs behind the request will be heard, and will be more likely to be heard as a request and not a demand; thus, clarity increases the likelihood that the recipient of a request will be willing to do it.

Elements of a Clear Request

The term *requests* as we use it here has one crucial distinction and three characteristics that define it. The basic distinction inherent in Nonviolent Communication Requests is that they are not demands— meaning there is no accompanying threat of physical or emotional force or negative consequences if the request is not agreed to. The three defining characteristics are that requests are doable, present tense, and stated in action language.

Practice Pause

Think of a request you have been wanting to make of someone, but have been putting off. What need do you think this request would fulfill? Connect with this need, then see if your thinking and energy around making the request shift.

Requests Versus Demands

The distinction between a request and a demand lies in our intention. We might use the same words to make either a request or a demand, but where are we coming from in making it? If we are asking someone out of "demand energy," then we are not making a request. In a request, the other person is free to turn down the request with no threat of negative consequences, immediate or in the future.

While we can try to be clear internally, before making a request, whether we are requesting or demanding, it is often only when we hear a no that we know for sure. If we then have any sense that we will try to punish the person for their no, perhaps by withholding something from them or turning down one of their requests, then we have in fact been making a demand. Seeking to induce shame, guilt, or depression for not agreeing to do what we want is a sure sign of a demand. (See Example 8 on facing page.)

Even when we are clear that we are making a request of a person, they may well hear it as a demand. You cannot control how your communication will be received; you can only control your intention and your actions—what you say and do. If a person does receive your request as a demand, your choices, after reconnecting with yourself, are to start with empathy or with expression. You can first guess what their need is (and perhaps what they might be feeling) based on what they said, and then renew your request. Or, you might start with expression, assuring the person that you are making a request and do not want them to agree unless they do so in order to meet their own needs. You might also combine the two responses; you might start with empathy, followed by expression and then your renewed request.

Moreover, if you are on the receiving end of the communication, you can choose to respond to demands as requests. This would entail first empathizing with yourself, and then silently guessing the needs of the speaker. With this preparation, you can decide whether to do what they are demanding or not, confident that you are doing so to meet your own needs. Or, you might empathize with the speaker out loud and say no through expressing what need of yours would not be met by saying yes.

Example 8

For some time now, you have been realizing that you would be interested in taking on some more responsibility in the projects you are assigned to. You decide to make a request of Magna, and in preparation for that, you spend some time getting clear on your needs and formulating the request. When you approach Magna and make your request, she responds by saying: "That's not going to work right now. Let's revisit it down the road sometime." You leave feeling angry, thinking: "She should have said yes. Can't she see that I'm up to the challenge? Next time she wants something, we'll just see."

As you hear these words in your head, you see that your request was really a demand. You do self-empathy, and when you've connected with the needs not met, you find the space to do silent empathy for Magna, and consider what needs she may have been meeting in saying no.

Doable Requests

To make a request doable seems simple enough, until we realize how often our requests of others are not doable. A boss saying to a subordinate, "You need to not take things so personally!" may sound on the surface like a reasonable request, but it is not doable. This request leaves out a crucial piece of information—what specific conduct does the boss anticipate would meet his need? A doable request might be, "The next time you're getting feedback on your project in the team meeting, would you be willing to reflect back your understanding of the feedback before you react?" This is a doable request that the boss might make, imagining that this might meet his needs for effectiveness and collaboration. Here are more examples of non-doable requests:

- Would you be reasonable?
- I'd like you to be more considerate.
- Could you please show me some appreciation?
- I just want you to feel good about this decision.
- Would you lighten up?
- Could you be more of a team player?
- Can't you just let go of the past?

Action-Language Requests

Formulating a request in action language means that we say what it is we want as opposed to what we don't want. Marshall Rosenberg tells a wonderful story illustrating the problem. To paraphrase, a wife is upset that her husband does not come home from the office until late, often after the kids have already gone to bed. She confronts him one evening, and concludes by saying, "Could you please just not spend so much time at the office?" The next week, the husband tells his wife he has signed up for a golf tournament so as not to spend so much time at the office. To his surprise, she is furious. As they work it out, it becomes clear that the following would have more clearly conveyed what she wanted: "Would you be willing to have dinner with the children and me here at six o'clock four nights a week, and spend some time with them before they go to bed?" (See Example 9 below.)

Often when we think of making a request, it stems first from noticing that somebody is doing something that we don't want. For example, you and your coworker get in an argument, and your coworker is speaking louder than you would like. Your first response might be, "Would you please stop yelling?" Again, this is an example of what you don't want—yelling. In this case, what is it that you do want? Maybe your request is "Would you be willing to speak at a volume level that matches what I'm using right now?" or "Would you be willing to be silent for the next minute?" If you notice that your request is stated in terms of what you do not want, take a minute to translate it into what you do want.

Example 9

You and Karen are co-planning work on a new project, and you think that she is intending to take all of what you consider the interesting work for herself, and leave what you view as the mundane tasks for you and the other team members. You decide to talk to her about it, and in order to do so, you first get clear on what your request is. You begin with "I want her to be more reasonable and stop taking all the interesting stuff for herself!" You realize how this is not doable, and that it is what you don't want instead of what you do want. You connect with your needs for respect and excitement about the work, and reframe your request. When you talk to Karen, you say, "Karen, would you be willing to sit down with me today to discuss how we can divide the work on the project in a way that allows all of us to feel excitement and contribution toward the project?" Karen agrees to discuss this with you.

Present Tense Requests

Requests, as we are talking about them here, are asking for what we want to happen right now. Nonetheless, the way our requests are phrased in everyday speaking, they often do not sound as if they are in the present tense. This generally works out fine as long as we are clear ourselves that our request is present tense. For example, we might say to someone, "Will you go to lunch with me on Wednesday?" or "Will you get the report in to me by five o'clock Friday afternoon?" The distinction is whether we are asking someone to do something in the future, or whether we are asking now for their present intention to do something in the future. We may use the same language, but it is helpful to be clear that what we are asking for is their present intention. Phrased in present time, the examples above would be, "Would you be willing now to set the intention to go to lunch with me on Wednesday?" and "Are you willing to agree now to get the report in to me by Friday afternoon at five o'clock?"

This may seem like a small distinction; however, clarity around the present tense nature of a request has an important consequence. If we are not clear with ourselves and with the other person that we are asking for a present intention to act, as opposed to a promise that some future action will take place, we may think we have an understanding about the agreement yet find that understanding is not shared by the other person. This can, and often does, lead to conflict when that future time arrives. We all know that life can get in the way of the best-laid plans. I may fully intend to go to lunch with someone next Wednesday, but I cannot guarantee that I will do it. Any number of situations may arise to prevent me; there may be a natural disaster, a personal or family crisis, or a less extreme situation that likewise precludes my fulfilling my original intention. If taken literally, asking someone to agree or promise to get the report to you by five o'clock on Friday is to ask someone to commit to something they do not have the physical capacity to guarantee will happen. Nonetheless, we do this all the time, and generally it works out fine. It can become problematic, however, when the party being asked does not trust the intention behind the request, either because they perceive themselves as having less power and therefore subject to punishment for failure, or because there is a history of conflict that has eroded trust. In these situations, both clarity within yourself about the distinction and the use of language that mirrors that distinction can be crucial.

Practice Pause

Think of a recent request you made of someone. What, if anything, needs to change for it to be doable, present tense, and in action language?

When I took on the practice of requests, I would often formulate the request in my head to make the present tense distinction clear: "Would you be willing to tell me that you have the present intention of going with me to lunch on Wednesday?" Then I might say to the person, "Would you go to lunch with me on Wednesday?" This silent practice helps me be clear that I am not actually asking them to be there, I am asking them to tell me their present intention to be there.

The beginning of my internal formulation of this request presents a good rule-of-thumb phrase to remember: if I start with "Would you be willing to tell me . . . ," then there is a good chance that my request will be present tense, doable, and in action language. In fact, sometimes when I'm not as clear as I would like to be about what my request is, I'll just start with "Would you be willing to tell me . . ." and try to fill in the words when I get there.

Categories of Requests

Requests can be divided into three categories: action requests and two types of process requests.

Action Requests

Action requests ask for a change in behavior, either from another person or from yourself. Here are some examples of action requests:

- Would you be willing to get me a glass of water?
- Would you hand me that report?
- Would you give me authorization to start this project?
- Would you be willing to assist me in this project by doing the following . . . ?

These are the requests that, if met, you imagine will meet your needs.

Process Requests

The two types of process requests ask a person to tell you either what they've just heard you say, or how they feel having heard what you've just said. Both of these are forms of action requests, yet they are treated as a separate category because they are often used in the process that leads up to the action request that was the focus or stimulus for the communication. (See Example 10 on page 58.)

When you ask a person to tell you how they feel having heard what you've said, you are in a sense seeking to measure the quality of the connection between you. The person's response will inform you whether their needs were met or not met in hearing you. For instance, if a person says, "I feel irritated hearing what you've said," you can be confident that their needs were not met, and you can follow up. Conversely, if they say they feel encouraged, then you can feel assured in continuing with the conversation. As is often the case, when you ask a person how they feel, they may tell you what they are thinking. You will still be able to get a sense of the quality of the connection between you, and again this assessment will inform what you next choose to say.

Practice Pause

Imagine how you might insert a process request into a conversation you had recently, or one that is upcoming.

When you ask a person to tell you what they heard you say, you can think of it as a means of assessing whether the message you sent was received as you intended it to be. In everyday parlance, we often ask people if they understand what we're saying. Unfortunately, if they say they do, we don't have a way of assessing whether they understand what we intend; they may have understood something quite different from what we wanted them to hear. Hence, developing the practice of asking other people to reflect what you've said, and also your own practice of reflecting what a person has said to you, will increase your confidence that you are understanding and being understood. Also, this practice will likely reveal how frequently the message you or someone else sends is misunderstood by the receiver.

Example 10

When you and Karen get together to talk through the division of work, you begin by expressing your concern. "Karen, I'd really like to feel excited and interested in the work we are doing, and certain parts of this project are more interesting to me than others. I'm confident that's true for you and everyone else on the team as well. I'd really like to find a way for us to make sure that everyone gets a chance to work on things that they find valuable." Because you would like to know whether Karen is on the same page with you, you decide to end with a process request: "I'm wondering how you feel hearing what I've just said?"

Data Collection Requests

There is a particular type of action request that can be especially helpful in the workplace, and that is a data collection request. These requests come in handy in situations where more information needs to be uncovered to make a clear request, and are often used when a request has something to do with another person's particular behaviors. In ongoing interactions between coworkers, there is sometimes something about the way one person interacts that the other does not enjoy. People might say, "It's just something about the way you act." Someone willing to be candid might say, "I can't put my finger on it, but you just seem rude and abrasive." Neither of these statements gives specific examples that tell the observation, and thus they offer little opportunity for clarity. Data collection requests are intended to move us toward clarity about what we observe, which will then lead to clarity about what other action requests we might make to get our needs met.

Since we can be on either side of this equation, let's look first at how data collection requests work when it is our actions that stimulate someone else. All of us have been in situations where everything we do seems to irritate or frustrate a coworker. Yet they may not be able to tell you in observation language what it is you do that stimulates their frustration or irritation, particularly when they do not know the distinctions of Nonviolent Communication. As a consequence, even if you are fortunate enough to get to this level of conversation, you still don't understand what it is you're doing, and you are therefore unable to choose whether or not to seek to change.

How might you facilitate this kind of data collection request? When it becomes clear that you are the stimulus for irritation, you might say: "When we interact, I get the sense that you're irritated. I would like to learn how our interactions could be easier for both of us. Would you be willing to spend five minutes with me right now to name what it is I do that you don't like?"

The response might be "I don't know what it is exactly. It's just something about your attitude." Your counter-response might be "Would you be willing to agree upon a process for us to identify examples of what it is you don't like as they arise in the future?"

In these kinds of situations, the request is often designed to get us toward where we would like to be in the future. If the person agrees to a process, your request might be this: "Next time you experience me doing the behavior we're discussing now, would you be willing to tell me, so that I can begin to understand what it is you don't like?" It may take several iterations of this request being played out, each time adding to the data set, for both parties to understand what is happening. After you've collected enough data, one of you may have an action request that would specify the desired change.

Thus far we've talked about a situation where someone else is bothered by your conduct and is not able to describe it in observation language. All of what we've said thus far is equally applicable to situations where you are bothered by a coworker's conduct that you're not able to describe such that they understand what you are talking about. Perhaps something about the tone of their voice when they speak to you, or their manner, irritates you. You might say something like this: "I'd like to talk to you about how we can interact more easily. Are you available and willing right now to take five minutes to start on this?" Assuming they are agreeable, you might say: "There's something about the way you interact with me that I don't enjoy. I'm at a loss to be able to name it for you so I can ask if you'd be willing to do it differently. I'm hoping you'd be willing to work out a way for us to learn together about what this is, as a step toward us being able to have an easier, more satisfying working relationship."

What you are working toward is an agreement with your coworker so that in the future, when this behavior arises, you can point it out and your coworker won't take it as criticism, just as data collection. Your request might be, "Next time I experience this discomfort, would you be willing to let me stop you and point out that what you are doing is an example of what I'm talking about right now?"

Practice Pause

In what situation in your workplace might a data collection request be helpful? Think about what that request might be and how you might make it.

These conversations, in any particular situation, might be much longer and more involved than the examples above. For instance, you might have a whole interaction and a series of process and action requests to organize the context within which you can broach your main subject. At that arranged session, again you might use the process requests of asking how the person feels about what you've said or asking them to tell you what they heard you say, all in order to establish connection and be confident that the message you're sending is the message they are receiving. This might all be a lead-up to the discussion about the reactions you are having to the conduct and your proposal for a data collection process to collaborate toward a mutually satisfying outcome.

Helping Others Formulate Clear Requests

Once you have practiced and learned how to formulate requests, you can lend your skills to others to help them make clear requests. This is particularly helpful when you are the recipient of the request and want to make sure that you have a shared understanding of what the person wants. The way I do this is to reflect back to the person what I have heard them request, except I insert language that is present tense, action oriented, and doable. This often also helps the other person gain clarity on what it is they want. In fact, this type of reflection has become almost second nature for me, in both work and personal interactions. I almost unconsciously reflect back what I'm hearing to make sure I'm hearing it the way they would like and to give them the assurance that they have been heard. We have already noted that most of us have not been trained in making requests; people will often want something and talk around it, without actually stating the request. If I get the sense or hear someone is trying to make a request, and I want certainty and clarity about it, then I may reflect my understanding of the request back to them. (See Example 11 on page 62.)

When making requests, we often use language that has a lot of assumptions. For instance, imagine your manager sees you walk into your workplace fifteen minutes after you agreed you would arrive and says, "What is your reason for being late again?" The assumption is that you are just now arriving at work. The truth may be that you arrived early and are returning from something work-related. Another example is asking someone, "What are you sad about?" instead of asking first, "Are you sad?" Our task in getting clear about our needs and requests and formulating doable, present tense, action-language requests is to have as few assumptions implicit in the request as possible. In this way, we increase the likelihood that we will be able to get our needs met and help others get theirs met through clear communication.

Example 11

You have stepped into Magna's office to ask a question, and while there, you fill her in on the project you and Karen are co-managing. Magna responds by saying, "That's great, keep me in the loop, would you?" She then takes a phone call, essentially dismissing you. As you leave, you realize that she has made a request, but you are not clear what it is she actually wants. Does she want some kind of regular update, by email or in person, or does she just want to know when milestones have been reached, or something else? You guess that her needs might be for inclusion and awareness of what's going on. In order to meet your need for understanding, you approach Magna after her call and say, "Magna, I'd like to understand better how you would like to be kept in the loop; would you be willing to tell me what specifically would do that?" She responds by saying: "Sure. Let me know if you need my help on anything, and also send me an email when you have completed each of the major stages that were laid out in the project proposal."

Chapter 6

Suggestions for Addressing Common Workplace Communication Challenges

When you have become more adept at the silent practices of awareness, self-empathy, and silent empathy laid out in Chapter 2, and as a result have gained more confidence, you may feel ready to start using these skills in more complex situations and including more of the out loud skills of empathy and expression in your communication. In this section, we'll discuss using Nonviolent Communication skills in situations that might present you with more challenge, when you are ready. We have included a myriad of perennially problematic workplace issues, including enemy images of yourself or others, difficult conversations, humor, prejudice, meetings, power differentials, gossip, feedback and evaluations, workplace cleanliness, broken agreements, email, and termination of employment.

Recognizing Enemy Images

Enemy image is a term I have borrowed from Marshall Rosenberg. I have an enemy image whenever I have a judgment, diagnosis, or analysis of someone else or myself as a thought in my head. I like to work with enemy images because I do not like how I feel going about my daily life when I have them. I also do not like how I act when I'm thinking in enemy images and experiencing the feelings that are consistent with having such thoughts.

These are examples of enemy images:

- She does not care.
- He is aggressive.
- They are out to get me.
- She is really smart.
- He is better than I.
- I screwed up.
- I am great.
- He is crazy.

All of these statements have a commonality—they put yourself or others into a static box labeled with who or what they are. I have heard this spoken about in a Buddhist context as having one side of the mind standing on the other.

As I see it, the two main problems with enemy images, besides how they make me feel and act, are that they dehumanize and they tend to create exactly what I don't want. By dehumanize, I mean that any time we label someone in a static way, we limit their full humanity and then tend to interact with them out of this diminished idea of who they are. In doing so, we often find our expectations are borne out. Marshall Rosenberg speaks to this point by saying, "You get what you see." For instance, if you go into a meeting with the expectation of a hostile reception, you will likely act and speak in ways that increase the likelihood that you will be received in the way you fear. As Claire Nuer, the founder of the Learning as Leadership process, said, "You create exactly what you don't want." (For more, see www.learnaslead. com.) By having a believed judgment about oneself or others, the mind will unconsciously sort information available to it in such a way as to support the believed judgment. In this way, the belief filters our perception and becomes a self-reinforcing mechanism—we get what we believe. (See Example 12 on page 66.)

Now, you might be thinking: "So what if I think my boss is a jerk? As long as I don't say or do anything to act on the thought, it doesn't matter." In my experience, however, it matters a lot. In the mediation work that I do, when I have a judgment in my head, I can see disconnection beginning to happen in the room within moments. I don't think that this is something metaphysical that passes through the ether or that's not explainable by science. Rather, I think we "leak" what we are thinking in ways that are subtly picked up by others. Whenever a person has a thought that they do not consciously disbelieve, their neurological system will release neurotransmitters that are consistent with that thought. Thus, our thoughts affect our feeling state, which in turn affects our micromovements, the rhythm of our speech, the words we choose, and the energy with which we deliver them. All of that together communicates on an unconscious level. This phenomenon explains why an unexpressed thought nonetheless has discernible physical consequences in the world. Most of us are aware that a large percentage of communication happens nonverbally. This should not be at all a surprise: as babies we are totally dependent for survival on the adults around us, and hence we learn to read people unconsciously from a very early age and continue to do so throughout our lives.

Why go to the trouble of doing the enemy image "process" I describe below—why not just think of something else or in some way banish the offending thought from your mind? I have not been successful using this approach. If I tell you, "Whatever you do, don't think of an elephant," you will almost assuredly have difficulty keeping thoughts of elephants from flooding your mind.

For many years I tried the approach of thinking of something else or just avoiding the undesired thought. My efforts included affirmations, prayer-like approaches, and concentration-based meditation practices. These would be helpful for a time, but then the thoughts would come back with renewed vigor. I have been more satisfied with the results of using the enemy image process. I like the immediate transformative effects; I like how I feel, and I like how I conduct myself—the consequences I foster in the world. In a way, the enemy image process acts like the goalie-magnet phenomenon in soccer. If a soccer player, running down the field, about to kick the ball toward the goal, looks at the goalie, they have increased the likelihood that they will kick the ball directly at the goalie. As a consequence, players are encouraged to focus their attention on a space in the goal where the goalie is not and where they want the ball to go. The enemy image process similarly refocuses our thoughts on where we want to be instead of on keeping away from the offending thoughts.

Moreover, I find that with subsequent iterations of the process with regard to the same topic, the frequency, intensity, and intrusiveness of the enemy images begin to wane. Growing evidence from the neuroscience world shows that memories are affected by the act of remembering. Each time we recall a memory into conscious awareness, it is modified to some greater or lesser extent. Perhaps this is the reason for the success I have found using the enemy image process. It makes sense to me that each time I revisit an issue with emphatic connection to my needs, I am changing the way I remember the stimulus of old hurts and patterns.

Example 12

After another team meeting, in which it seems to you that Harold has dominated the discussion, you return to your office feeling grumpy. Your thoughts run something like this: "Harold is such a pain. He's always taking over everything and pretending to be boss, like he knows something we don't. He's so domineering and competitive." At these words, you realize that you have an enemy image of Harold—your thoughts are judgmental and diagnostic.

The Enemy Image Process

Once we are clear that we want to work with enemy images, the process is similar to other Nonviolent Communication processes. The first step is awareness: to realize that I have such judgments. The idea behind the enemy image process is that if I'm having a judgment, it is an expression of unmet needs. In doing this process, I shift to evaluating whether my needs are met or not. If I can translate the judgment into the needs not met, I will have tapped into the power of the mind, once directed to what is desired, to diligently search for strategies that will meet my needs.

This is not an analytical process; instead, ask the question gently, perhaps with a list of needs in front of you. In a musing frame of mind, query yourself as to whether it might be this need or that need. This is typically an iterative process in which the self-inquiry is repeated over and over again; with each response, you use changes in your felt sense to guide you in further guesses as to what the need might be.

Self-empathy and silent empathy are the central components to the enemy image process. First I get my need for empathy met by identifying the need or needs that I'm seeking to meet by making a judgment. If I'm having a judgment of somebody else, then I practice silent empathy, which shifts the focus of my attention onto the needs of the other person by guessing what needs they might be seeking to meet by the conduct that I am judging. Again, I do not have to be "right" about my guesses; the important thing is that I focus my attention on their needs as the motivation for their conduct. I am satisfied with this part of the process when I feel a certain resonance with my guess, and often this is accompanied by a marked change in my felt sense—in other words, I feel a shift. (See Example 13 on page 69.)

Practice Pause

Choose a recent judgmental thought of yourself or someone else, like "I screwed up" or "That person is impossible." While holding that thought in your mind, ask yourself, "What need am I seeking to meet by having that thought?"

Strategies to get your needs for empathy met include working with somebody else. The person helping you might make guesses as to what needs of yours are not met, or you might role-play the situation, with your companion role-playing you or the other person. If you work with someone else, I am confident that you will be more satisfied if you find someone you trust not to believe the judgments that you're having about yourself and the other person(s); someone who's had enough experience to hear the judgments but not take them as truth. You can then say, for example, "I just have this sense that he is an uncaring, insensitive creep," and you won't hear some version of this statement days or weeks later, as if what you said were reality. As I conceive of it, the judgment may be my starting point—I realize that that is what I am holding in my head—but I'm longing to translate it, and I want to be with someone who understands that translation process. In a sense, they need to be able to not believe my thoughts.

Role-playing can be used at a later stage in the process as well. Once I've been able to identify the need that I'm seeking to meet by making this judgment, and I've also connected with my guess as to the other person's needs, I may want to use role-playing as a way to practice an interaction with this person. With myself again playing either part, I can then gain some experience in interacting in a way that I would like. (If you have two people to practice with, you can take the role of observer at first if you feel more comfortable doing so.) I might even develop a script of what I would like to say to this person, give to my role-playing partner the script of what I most fear hearing back, and then practice my responses. This also gives me a chance to practice in-the-moment self-empathy, as I am likely to be triggered by hearing what I most fear.

The roles you choose to play in role-playing scenarios will likely meet different needs. For instance, if you play the other person, you're likely to gain greater insight into, and even compassion for, the needs motivating their actions. This is particularly so if the person playing you is consistently reflecting their guesses of your character's feelings and needs. If you play yourself, with the other reflecting their guesses of your feelings and needs, your need for empathy is likely to be met.

If you play yourself and your companion plays the other person as you suspect they might actually act, you will get practice responding to the reactions you most fear, meeting your need for trust in your ability to respond as you would like. Understanding what you need can help you choose which role-playing scenario will support you.

Example 13

Even though a part of you feels like your judgmental thoughts about Harold are right, you realize that these thoughts are creating distress in you, so you decide to use the enemy image process. You close your eyes and ask yourself, "What need of mine is not met when I think about Harold in this way?" After trying a few possibilities, you realize your need for connection isn't met by those thoughts. Then you ask, "What needs of mine are not met when I think about Harold's conduct in our last meeting?" Again, you go through a few ideas before hitting on those needs that feel closest for you: respect for your ability, and collaboration. Connecting with these needs, you then wonder what needs Harold might be meeting through his behavior. You think he might be acting out of needs for respect, to be heard, and for contribution.

Enemy Images at Work

In the workplace, the opportunity to use the enemy image process comes up frequently. For example, you might have an interaction with a coworker that results in hurt feelings on both sides. In thinking about reengaging with that person, you become aware of having judgmental thoughts. You might want to use the enemy image process so that when you do attempt to reengage, you will not be leaking your judgments through your body language, words, and tone of voice. Since your need for empathy will have been met, you will be more likely to be able to listen to the other person before needing to be heard yourself. Marshall Rosenberg refers to this as "empathy before education." Stephen Covey points to the same phenomenon in his book *The Seven Habits of Highly Effective People.* His fifth habit is "Seek first to understand, then to be understood." We are more likely to get our needs met when we are sufficiently open to hearing and connecting with the needs of others, when we help them get their need for empathy met before we try to express ourselves.

Practice Pause

Think of three specific instances from your workplace when the enemy image process would have come in handy.

Another prime situation for using the enemy image process is in relation to a boss. When someone has authority over us—when their conduct can affect our well-being and our needs for sustainability through continuing employment—we often hold certain beliefs and judgments about them. These judgments can affect how we interact, and using the enemy image process helps keep our communication from becoming muddied with our fears and beliefs.

Handling Difficult Conversations

We all face difficult conversations in the workplace: criticism from our boss, a conflict with a client, a coworker we find irritating, a subordinate who submits incomplete work—all might entail a conversation we do not look forward to having. When we anticipate that an interaction might be complicated, there are steps we can take to engage with the other person in ways that are more likely to be satisfying. We might think about this in three stages: preparing for the conversation, having it, and then learning from it afterward. These three stages may then repeat, much like the learning cycle we discussed in Chapter 3. If you find that there is an ongoing difficulty in having the kind of connection and relationship you would like to have with a person, you might cycle through these three stages again and again, learning more each time.

The preparing stage involves making sure that you have done your enemy image work ahead of time. If you anticipate that the conversation will be difficult, you might well have judgments and analyses of the person based on past interactions. Doing the enemy image process—giving yourself empathy for your judgments and doing silent empathy for the other person—can help you transform the intense emotional charge you might otherwise have going into the conversation, a charge that will tend to create exactly what you don't want. This is particularly true when you have thoughts that you want to make sure you don't act on. For example, some part of you may believe that the other person is not treating you fairly. If you simply think, "Well, I don't want to say anything about them not treating me fairly," you have actually increased the likelihood that your judgment will leak out in some way. In doing the enemy image process, you rehumanize the person and connect with your own needs.

In preparation, you also may want to practice having the conversation with someone else in a role-play. You can tell the other person what you imagine would be difficult for you to hear from the person, and then in the role-play take the time to give yourself empathy, do silent empathy, then formulate a response. In practice this may take a few minutes, but you will still be learning in-the-moment reaction skills by slowing it down—skills that may well serve you during the actual conversation.

Practice Pause

Think of a difficult conversation that you have been avoiding. Go through the preparation process, and see how you feel then about having the conversation.

Right before having the conversation, you might want to plan in some time to do self-empathy. Typically, there will be an upwelling of concerns and anxieties before going into a difficult situation; planning a self-empathy session around your reaction to anticipating the conversation, especially with a support person, can help you be present when you go into it. Setting an intention for the conversation ahead of time will also help. You can keep your intention fresh in your mind during the conversation by writing it on a three-by-five card, your hand, or your notepad.

You might well have planned how you want to start, and you may have role-played various versions of the conversation, but in the actual conversation, you want to be as present as possible and not rely on a script that cannot be true to the present moment. Holding your intention foremost in your mind instead of a planned script will help you maintain the kind of spontaneity and flow that the other person is likely to expect from you. If you are able to do self-empathy during the conversation, it can help by keeping you present to your needs; however, when first learning, it may be more than enough challenge to simply be in the conversation with as much presence as you can muster.

I have found it is best to anticipate that after the conversation, there's going to be a flood of judgmental thoughts about yourself, the other person, and the situation—try to schedule a time to do empathy. During this time, you can celebrate the needs met and mourn the needs not met in thinking about what happened during the conversation, and you can guess the needs of the other person. You can then shift into figuring out and naming what you learned. In this learning, you might replay how the conversation went, either in your head or again in a role-play with someone else—but replay it as you would like it to have happened. In this way, you are creating neural networks that store the information in the brain in a way that makes it more readily available when you are next in a similar situation. After going through this process, you then think about the next step, if there is one. As you plan for that step, if it includes another conversation, you cycle back to the first stage of preparation.

Addressing Humor in the Workplace

After I cofounded a law firm, and we grew into a twenty-person organization, I became more conscious of the management aspects of my work. Part of this was trying to figure out how to deal with humor. One of our associate attorneys, who had been with us from early on, used to tell very ribald jokes. Blonde jokes, Italian jokes (her husband's family was originally from Italy), other ethnic jokes, she would tell pretty much any joke. This was in the latter half of the 1980s and into the '90s, when there were a number of appellate cases in the United States arising out of claims by plaintiffs that they had been subjected to a hostile workplace: employees had brought actions against their companies after taking offense at the humor used by other employees and when management either participated in the humor or was unresponsive to complaints.

I did not want to stop my colleague from telling jokes, as it was clear to me that she and others (including myself) were enjoying themselves. I also trusted where her heart was, as I never saw her intentionally hurt someone or make any particular person the brunt of a joke. I was not concerned about a hostile workplace, but I was concerned that someone new who had not developed a relationship with this woman might be upset and not feel safe or comfortable expressing that they didn't enjoy the jokes she told on a regular basis.

Another aspect of humor that concerned me was my own use of humor, which was quite different from the kinds of jokes our associate attorney told. I had been raised in a family and school culture where sarcasm was used as a way of communicating displeasure and directives to comply with the social norm. I became aware that my own form of humor relied a lot on irony, on two meanings playing against each other with some ambiguity as to the intended one. For example, if I thought someone had done a good job in preparing a brief, I might say something like, "Well that brief really screwed the pooch!" I had a resistance to saying, "I really want you to know I appreciated that brief and thought it did what I wanted it to do" (partly because I didn't have that language at the time), so I would use this backhanded kind of humor to get my point across. Thus, my humor was very situational and topical. Eventually, I realized that given my role as one of the founding partners, the person who literally signed people's paychecks and conducted annual reviews, employees tended to misinterpret my humor; though I was clear within myself that I intended the benign meaning in my humor, employees tended to believe I meant the other one. Over and over again, they would report that their feelings were hurt by something I had said.

Practice Pause

How do you use humor? What is your intention in using it?

As a manager, then, I developed strategies for dealing with humor. I stopped using humor at all myself because of my experience with employees misunderstanding my intention; I concluded that everybody else could tell jokes, but I couldn't use my kind of in-the-moment humor. In response to the attorney who told ribald jokes, I decided that I would take any new employees aside and talk to them, letting them know that if there was anything about the jokes this person told that they felt uncomfortable about, I hoped they would say something— ideally to her, but if not, at least to me. I was pretty satisfied with these strategies, except for the fact that I didn't get to express the kind of humor I wanted to express.

Then I started learning Nonviolent Communication, and at one of the trainings I attended, I had the insight that I can only control my own intention and my own conduct, that I have no control over other people. Thus, if I am going to use humor, I first want to be clear about my own intention—I only want to come from an intention to fulfill my need for fun and play. My guess is that if I have any other intention in using humor, such as an intention to instruct, or any sense of wanting to punish, criticize, or undermine anyone with my humor, it is more likely to trigger a reaction in somebody else.

Even with my intention being to fulfill needs for fun and play, however, other people may still be distressed by my humor. For example, I mentioned in Chapter 2 a training I facilitated that included some people who had become friends of mine while participating in prior NVC workshops, and whom I hadn't seen in some time. We were doing a lot of playing around and telling jokes and teasing one another in the training, and another participant became very distressed. I was very clear about my intention in using humor, and I trusted my friends' intentions, and even so, my guess is that due to the other participant's history, she didn't feel safe. If, as in this case, I know that someone is not enjoying my humor, or if I suspect this based on clues such as their body language and what they are saying or not saying, I want to be willing to check. I can then use my skills to reconnect with them through empathizing with what needs of theirs may not be met.

If I feel uncomfortable with the jokes someone else is telling, I want to first be clear what needs of mine are not met. Then I can guess what needs the joke teller might be seeking to meet. In doing that, I may not have any reason to actually ask them to do anything different. For example, I may guess that they are meeting their need for fun and play, and their strategy just happens to be a stimulus for a reaction that comes out of my own life experience; I may just choose to deal with it on my own.

If, however, the joking continues to be a stimulus, or I suspect that they are trying to meet some need that I don't feel good about meeting with humor, I may want to say something to them. In speaking up about my discomfort, I am more likely to be heard in the way I would like if I can come from the energy that they are not doing anything wrong; they are just trying to meet a need. Thus, it really helps to mourn the needs not met when hearing the jokes, and to connect with some guess of what need they are meeting. In this way, I humanize the person, even while I continue to dislike the strategy they are using to meet the need. (See Example 14 below.)

I have had a hard time with certain jokes based on a derogatory view of particular groups of people—ethnic groups, women, and even lawyers. Based on the situation and my knowledge of a person, I might guess that someone telling a derogatory joke about an ethnic group is trying to meet their need for companionship. Even so, I believe those kinds of jokes have an effect that I don't like, so I may still want to say something—to educate the joke teller that I don't enjoy those jokes without making the person wrong or bad for telling them. After doing self- and silent empathy, I might bring it up with the joke teller by saying: "Remember you told that joke yesterday at lunch? I didn't want to tell you at the time because I just want this to be between us, but I felt really uncomfortable. When I think about telling jokes like that, I think it has an effect on us. It doesn't contribute to creating the kind of mutual respect of all beings in the world that I would like to have. I would like all people to have respect for one another." Then I would end with one of the process requests, either asking how they feel hearing me say that or asking them to tell me what they heard so I can make sure I'm getting my message across in the way I would like.

Example 14

Harold comes in after lunch one day and says to you and Karen: "Hey, I just heard a new joke. Want to hear it?" Without waiting for an answer, he continues:

"Why did the disabled man get washed in the kitchen sink? Because that's where you are meant to wash vegetables!" Harold laughs as you cringe inside, and you notice Karen rolling her eyes. You feel a sense of revulsion because you need consideration for the sensibilities of others. This is not the first time Harold has told a joke that has been very uncomfortable for you to hear. As the result of your off-line self- and silent empathy sessions after those prior times, you feel ready to say something now. You start by guessing what need Harold was seeking to meet by telling the joke. You say: "So, Harold, help me understand what you are getting at with this joke. Did you tell it to create a connection with Karen and me? Or maybe did you just want to have some fun?"

"Yeah, don't you like the joke?" Harold asks in response.

"Well, actually, I feel a little uncomfortable when I hear jokes like this because I need consideration for the feelings of others. How do you feel hearing what I just said?"

"I feel like you just don't know how to take a joke," Harold retorts. You respond by saying, "So, are you wanting to have companions to have fun with?"

"Yeah, what is wrong with that?"

"Nothing. I would like to get to have fun and joke with you too. I just would like to do it in a way that is not at the expense of others. Would you be willing to figure out how we could do both?"

Harold replies, "Well, I guess so."

Practice Pause

Think of a time when someone's use of humor stimulated discomfort in you. Give yourself empathy. When your need for empathy is met, use silent empathy and then consider what you might have said at the time.

Challenging Prejudice in the Workplace

As the increase in "diversity training" in workplaces attests, prejudice can be one of the more difficult workplace issues to confront. The belief that we or other people are being discriminated against based on our race, class, gender, sexual orientation, or any other category can bring up strong reactions and deep-seated emotions related to basic needs for survival and respect for who we are.

The term *prejudice* is commonly used to refer to certain types of behavior and thinking, and while everyone generally understands what it means, I find it a problematic word to use. I find that using it to judge someone else's or your own conduct is not likely to get you what you want. To tell someone else they are prejudiced or call ourselves prejudiced in our own head is probably going to set up a reactive pattern that does not lead to learning.

As far as I can tell, we all exhibit prejudice to the extent that we have enemy images about particular individuals and particular groups of individuals. Enemy images, remember, include not only negative judgments, but also all kinds of positive associations, such as thinking that one group is better than another group.

It is not difficult to become aware of our own enemy images, especially those that apply across groups of people. I know that I feel uncomfortable about my reactions to seeing certain people on the street late at night. I do not have concerns about my safety if I see a guy walking down the street carrying a briefcase and reading a newspaper.

If I see three teenage boys, however, using foul language and bouncing off of one another as they come toward me on the same side of the street in an industrial part of town, I have a different reaction. Skin color, ethnicity, social class, gender, education levels, the way people speak and the language they use, clothing and body piercings and tattoos, and the environment all affect my reactions to the people I encounter in different situations. Civil rights leader Jesse Jackson makes the point this way: "There is nothing more painful to me at this stage in my life than to walk down the street and hear footsteps and start thinking about robbery—then look around and see somebody white and feel relieved."

I am uncomfortable about my own reactions because they run counter to values that I hold. Research continues to show, however, that we all have these deep-seated biases, which are often linked to strong emotions. They also start early: "Many of our implicit associations about social groups form before we are old enough to consider them rationally. . . . a 2006 study . . . shows that full-fledged implicit racial bias emerges by age six—and never retreats."[1] We continue to hold these biases, formed based on our socialization before we are even aware of it, and even act out of them unless we can find a way to consciously counteract these tendencies.

Since acting on our implicit biases is likely to be counter to our values, our first impulse may be to try to get rid of these thoughts. I have not been successful in telling myself not to be prejudiced or not to react in a certain way. My reactions are always immediate, preceding any thought about them. What I can do is notice them when they arise. I can then be more open to placing myself in a position to gather additional information to test my preconceptions, as long as I can do so in safety. Most of the time that I do this, I find that the information I get belies my assumptions, and I've grown to enjoy having the opportunity to prove that my reactive perception is inaccurate. In doing so over and over again, I become more sensitive to my reactive

---

1. Siri Carpenter, "Buried Prejudice: The Bigot in Your Brain," *Scientific American*, April 2008, http://www.scientificamerican.com/article.cfm?id=buried-prejudice-the-bigot-in-your-brain&page=3.

judgments, and I am much more open to learning about the people I come in contact with and connecting with them as human beings, instead of merely as representatives of a group.

Practice Pause

What are your own implicit biases? When are you aware of these biases operating?

Someone else may also do something that I judge as displaying prejudice; however, if I frame it this way, I am now in conflict with them. Since disconnection and being in conflict are unlikely to create what I want, my desire is to create connection. To do this, I again use the basic distinctions. I want to be clear what it is the person said or did—the observation—that I then judged. When I am clear on the observation, I can look for the needs of mine that are not met. When I deeply connect with my own needs, I might then be able to shift to being curious about what was motivating the other person when they said or did what I found objectionable. After silent empathy, I might decide to engage with them from a place where I'm clear that it is not about them being wrong. From there, I can express the pain that is stimulated in me in a way less likely to be heard as criticism; I can let them know that my distress is about me, and wonder aloud if we can work it out so they can meet their needs in some other way.

For instance, on more than one occasion, men that I have had business dealings with have spoken about women in ways that I find distressing: referring to particular women by anatomical features, imputing sexual promiscuity, or assessing desirability. Hearing these comments stimulated distress and intense discomfort because of my desire for all beings to be treated with consideration and respect. Moreover, I have typically been somewhat confused, as the language seemed to me to be inconsistent with what I understood were the person's true sentiments about the women in their lives.

Often I have been at a loss as to what to say in the moment; typically I have been nonplussed into silence and have done my reconnection work of self- and silent empathy away from the speaker. That reconnection has involved the learning cycle and practice either in my mind or with a support person to develop what I might say should the situation arise again. My goal is to be in integrity with my values and at the same time to connect and demonstrate my caring for the well-being of the speaker. In one particular instance, after hearing one of these distressing statements, I started the conversation with the speaker by saying, "Hold on a second. I would like to let you know something. When you refer to that woman that way, I feel really uncomfortable because I want people to be treated with respect. Would you let me know if you are OK with me saying this to you?" This led to a very connected conversation with the speaker, one in which I learned that he was using that language as an attempt to connect with me. When he could hear that I preferred he use different language to reach his goal of connection, he quite readily and without resistance shifted to that approach. The upshot of this set of interactions resulted in us being closer together than we had been initially.

Practice Pause

Think back to a recent time when you perceived someone acting from prejudice. Do the enemy image process, and then consider what you might say should a similar situation arise.

If the action that you believe to be prejudiced is directed at you, it may take a good deal of empathy before you are willing or able to consider the other person's motivations. Going deeply into this process can move you out of your reaction—whether it is depression, hopelessness, or rage—and bring healing. Enlisting someone else who is knowledgeable about the process of empathy can aid you in staying with the needs and associated feelings that come up, and not reverting to the story and the perceived injustice.

Contributing to Effective Meetings

In most workplaces, meetings in one form or another take place, often to discuss and decide on policy, product, or direction. I have been in meetings that provided forward movement, used time in a way I liked, and also created a sense of camaraderie and teamwork. And I have been in countless meetings that became a source of frustration and disconnection. Even if you are not a facilitator of a meeting, there are ways that you can help meetings become more satisfying to you by using a few key skills that help you stay connected, and help focus and clarify what people want.

While some people speak with clarity and succinctness, others seem to talk in order to find out what they want to say. In a meeting, this can draw out the conversation past the point where I am willing to continue to be engaged. When someone has talked for longer than you enjoy listening, you might want to interrupt. Usually, interruption is seen as "rude" and creates disconnection; however, there is a way to interrupt that instead can bring us together.

If you are clear that your needs are not being met in continuing to listen, first get clear on what needs you will meet by interrupting. For example, I often interrupt because I would like clarity about what a person is saying, or because I would like to know what they want. Knowing your needs helps you know what you will ask; the person speaking may initially be irritated when you interrupt, so you will want to have a specific connecting request ready, perhaps even tied to your needs. For example, you might ask the speaker to let you and the group know what they want done with the information being given, which is essentially asking the person to clarify their request. You might also reflect back what you have heard this person say, which can help them correct or hone in on the gist of their message.

One way to stay connected with what anyone in a meeting is saying is to look for whether they are saying either please or thank you. I find it helpful to operate out of the view that we speak either because we have a request of some sort, or because we are expressing thanks. If you think someone is saying please, you can try to guess the request if it is not clear. As we've already noted in Chapter 5, we are not taught how to make clear requests, and helping others do so is a key way you can contribute in a meeting. You might ask questions to help formulate a doable, present tense, action-language request, and ask the speaker to whom specifically they would like to direct their request. Especially when speaking to a group, it helps if a request is not left hanging with a general assumption that somebody will fulfill it.

For example, a number of years ago, I was working closely with another person, and when we had in my mind reached a conclusion, I would say, "We'll do that." After some time of working together, this person turned to me and said, "Who is this Will person?" This was many years before meeting Marshall Rosenberg and being exposed to Nonviolent Communication; nonetheless, it exemplifies the lack of clarity on my part regarding who was actually going to do what I understood had just been decided on. Helping others in a group clarify their requests helps get those requests met, which builds rapport and trust within the group.

Listening for people's appreciation and supporting more explicit expressions of thank you within a group typically produces results that I like. Taking the time to acknowledge and celebrate both individual and group accomplishments helps build group cohesion and in general increases individual satisfaction.

Practice Pause

Think about a recent conversation. Was the other person saying please or thank you? If they were saying please, how might you have helped them clarify their request?

Listening for please and thank you and helping others clarify requests helps you stay connected when others are speaking. When you have the floor, using process requests can help you stay connected with others and ensure that you are heard in the way you would like. If you are unsure whether you have been understood, you might ask for someone to tell you what they heard you say. When you get a sense from people's body language that perhaps they do or do not like what you are saying, you might ask them to report on how they feel about what you've said. The answers to these questions can help you decide what to say next. Finally, knowing why you are saying what you are saying and making a clear request helps you make your communication succinct and more likely to be well-received.

When people get frustrated in a meeting, they often speak out of their irritation, making demands of the group. This often happens when some kind of group decision-making process is employed and it doesn't meet someone's need for efficiency. Unfortunately, what I have experienced is that when someone expresses their anger in irritation and demands, it often slows down the process considerably, as it encourages others to express their frustration. If we sense something is happening in the group that is not meeting our needs, the best way to help the group is to do our own self-empathy first, so we are not reacting from our judgments. After getting in touch with the needs not met for us, we might then be able to guess what needs others are acting out of and find a way to make a request of the group that comes out of a connection with needs.

I was once in a conference plenary session when an argument broke out among a number of key people in the audience stimulated by a question the facilitator had asked. As the argument continued, with people getting more attached to their viewpoints, I felt increasingly uncomfortable. I began to do self-empathy when I noticed thoughts like "This argument is wasting our time, they are off the point." I then translated what was happening into Observations, Feelings, and Needs. As I stepped out of the judgments, more space opened up in me, and I began to consider what strategies might meet my needs, as well as the needs of others in the room who also might not be enjoying the direction of the conversation.

Though I was not one of the senior members of this community, I interrupted and said I was uncomfortable with what was happening, and that I wanted to understand whether it was contributing to the facilitator's question. I then turned to the facilitator and asked him, "Would you be willing to tell us, of all that has been said in response to your question, what has been helpful to you?" After a moment of stunned silence, he turned to a woman who had responded early on and said that nothing had been helpful except for what she had said. Since her comment had nothing to do with the topic of the argument, the room shifted, and the conversation moved on in directions that I enjoyed far more. Doing my own self-empathy helped me find a strategy that contributed to the meeting; had I intervened before I had done my own work, my question would more likely have come out of my judgments, and would likely have stimulated responses I would not have enjoyed.

As we said in Chapter 2, even if you do not feel comfortable speaking up in a group, just doing the silent practices of self- and silent empathy can contribute to a meeting. To be constantly connecting with your own and others' needs changes the dynamic of a group whether you open your mouth or not. If you are relatively new to these skills, or if you notice that you have trouble maintaining your focus, you can practice by jotting down Observations, Feelings, and Needs on a notepad during the meeting. At the very least, this practice can help you shift quickly out of thoughts of irritation; at best, it can reconnect you with your own needs and influence any requests or actions you take in the group.

Navigating Power Differentials

People often report to me that they perceive power differences in the workplace. Of course, there are some real power differences; the power to sign a paycheck and the power to fire a person are very real. These real differences, however, often get expanded out in ways that do not seem accurate to me. In other words, people often perceive that a person has power over them and that therefore they cannot make a request for a change, and do not actually check that assumption. Needs for safety and security of livelihood get in the way of approaching a person who is perceived to hold power. Nonetheless, it becomes self-defeating to feel your needs are not being met, yet not reveal those needs and make a request that you think would meet them. Ironically, when I was a boss and in that position of power, I often felt powerless in hearing people "complain"; I felt how little power I had to affect the world. My powerlessness came out of not being clear what it was that would be a satisfying outcome for the others involved as well as for me. Since the people around me typically did not make requests to meet their needs, I was left to mediate between myself and what I imagined might be the other person's requests and needs. These were rarely as clear to me as the other person seemed to think they ought to be.

I see two different contexts in which you might perceive a power differential. In one context, you think the person might not know that your needs are not being met, or you are unsure whether he knows. In the other context, you are fairly confident the person knows your needs aren't met, but cannot imagine how to meet her needs and also meet yours; therefore she is not as sensitive to your needs as you would like. The response in either situation is the same; however, you might need additional empathy in the latter case. We tend to get highly triggered when we think that someone knows our needs are not being met but is doing nothing about it. Of course, we can never be sure unless we check whether the person knows or not, but in order to get to the point where we can even think of doing that, we may need other people to help us get our need for empathy met.

The section on "Handling Difficult Conversations" describes the core process to use in cases of power differentials. I encourage you to place particular emphasis on preparing for the conversation. Doing our own self-work of getting clear about our needs helps relieve the agitation and angst that often accompanies these situations. Without doing the self-work, we are more likely to present our request in a way that the other person will hear as not respecting their autonomy. After doing our own work, we then can present our request in a way that has more clarity and openness to it.

Of course, Nonviolent Communication is not a magic wand that you can wave when you are afraid that the person you are talking with will not receive you in the way that you would like. NVC processes and skills can help you get connected in a way where you will act out of greater clarity, which increases the likelihood that you will get the hoped-for response. However, you also might not. In these situations, self- and silent empathy can still help you get reconnected with your needs in a way that allows you to think more clearly about the situation. You might then find other ways to get your needs met, or decide that you need to remove yourself from the situation, but you will be able to do so in a way that maintains connection with yourself and those around you. (See also the section on "Transforming the End of Employment," starting on page 104.)

Responding When Colleagues Complain

We have all experienced it—you go to get some water or coffee as part of a bio-break, and two colleagues are there, speaking in muted (or not so muted) tones, complaining about somebody or rehashing the latest office gossip. All too soon, one of the participants seeks to draw you into the conversation. You find yourself in the unpleasant position of not wanting to engage in gossip, yet also not wanting to reject the overture for inclusion. (See Example 15 on the next page.)

Example 15

As you walk into the kitchen to get your lunch, you notice Harold and Karen suddenly drop their voices, then look relieved. "We thought you might be Magna," they laugh uncomfortably. Karen says: "We were just talking about this latest memo. Can you believe it? I mean, telling us that all office supplies down to a single paper clip have to be approved? Who does she think she is?" Harold turns to you, "Don't you think she's being a total tightwad?" You are aware of the silence as they wait for you to confirm the diagnosis.

I generally distinguish two types of gossip: one in which someone passes on a story about someone else, embedded with judgments; and another in which someone talks about an interaction they had with someone else, again with embedded judgments of the other person. It is my guess that two different things are going on with these different types of gossip. When people repeat gossip about another person, they are attempting to establish common norms or see if you share their same set of values. Whispering about so-and-so's teenage daughter's pregnancy or recounting the suspicion that the guy from accounting is stealing office supplies are in this category. In the other type, when someone is telling about an interaction they had with someone else, the speaker is trying to measure their sense of reality. They want to check their perspective with someone else: do others see that what this person did is outrageous? It is a way of calibrating their norm. I think what we are really seeking with this second type of gossip is empathy—we want our pain to be heard. In getting the other person to agree with our judgments, we get a kind of empathy, but not a fully satisfying one, as we have not yet connected to our needs.

When encountering either of these forms of gossip in the workplace, you have a number of options from the perspective of Nonviolent Communication. You can choose to see this as an opportunity to practice the silent skills of NVC. It may help to start from the viewpoint that the person engaging in gossip is most likely expressing their pain through stating judgments of others. You may want to begin with self-empathy, and thereby reconnect with your own needs that are not met in the conversation. You might then find yourself switching to silent empathy, being with the other person and silently translating what they are saying into the possible needs behind their evaluations, analyses, or diagnoses. Again, through both of these processes, you are altering your thoughts, which has the effect of altering how you feel about the situation. As a result, you are altering your body language, what you say, and how you say it. All of this combined can have a powerful impact on your felt sense and on those around you, without you having to use NVC out loud.

What I have found in these situations, however, is that if you are silent, others will want to draw you into the conversation, so you might also want to practice ways to respond in case this happens. I would suggest you try for a response that is in alignment with your values but also seeks connection with the person asking you the question. For example, if your coworker tells you a rumor about how the manager recently took credit for another person's work, and asks you, "Didn't you just know that he's a total fraud?" you might respond with empathy: "Are you angry because you'd like to know that the managers here have some integrity?"

You can also respond with some combination of expression and empathy. If someone has recounted a story and ended by asking you, "Isn't he being a jerk?" you might respond with something like this: "Well, I feel uncomfortable calling him a jerk because that doesn't meet my needs for consideration to think of him that way, but I'm wondering if what's going on for you is also a need for respect and consideration, and those needs aren't met when this person acts in the way you've described?" This is an example of using NVC to first express my Feeling ("discomfort") and Need ("consideration") in response to the Observation ("calling him a jerk"), followed by a Request. The request in this instance is an empathy guess as to what the other person's needs are ("respect and consideration") in response to the stimulus or observation ("when this person acts in the way you've described"). (See Example 16 on the next page.)

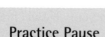

Practice Pause

Recall a recent situation in which people engaged in gossip or complaints about others. Imagine how you might have responded, beginning with self- and silent empathy.

These examples are not intended to be magic scripts that will get you the response you want every time. I have found that with the intention to create connection and the use of NVC principles, I increase the likelihood that what I say will produce the connection I am seeking. In any particular instance, however, I cannot be sure that the other person will respond as I would like. If I do stimulate a reaction that leaves me feeling overwhelmed or stuck as to my response, I may take the option of a time-out (see "Taking the Time You Need," in Chapter 4).

Example 16

You take a deep breath and become conscious of how you feel about the memo. You realize that you feel angry because your needs for respect and a certain level of trust in your own honesty are not being met. You decide to respond with empathy to Harold and Karen, hoping that their evaluations are coming from similar unmet needs. "It sounds like you are upset because you would like management to show that they trust you, and this memo seems to indicate the opposite. Is that what's going on for you?"

Giving Feedback and Evaluations

We encounter feedback in a number of ways in the workplace. When working with another person or group of people to deliver goods or services, feedback is a key component to being able to continually correct toward the goal. Feedback is also institutionalized in the annual or semiannual evaluation process featured in many workplaces.

Feedback is often one of the most problematic pieces of communication, whether you are on the giving or receiving end, and whether it is in relation to someone at your level or above or below you in the office hierarchy. It often brings up our needs for safety and security, occurring as it does in relationship to our livelihood.

All too often what we call feedback is loaded with judgments about the other person or ourselves. It inherently contains implications of right and wrong, good and bad, and it reinforces the use of labels to define who we are, limiting the full scope of our humanity. We tend to like these labels when we perceive them as positive, and dislike them otherwise. These statements are often both said and received as "truth." Examples of feedback in this vein sound like this:

- You messed up again.
- I don't ever do this right.
- You're an outstanding employee.
- Your work on this project is unacceptable.
- You need to pay more attention to detail.
- You're not detail-oriented.
- You're careless.
- It's important for your advancement here to be able to see the big picture.
- You need to be able to work more compatibly with other people.
- You are a great communicator.
- You need to be more aware of other people's feelings.
- You need to stop being so sensitive.
- It's imperative that you learn to communicate with others better.
- I just received another report of you being inconsiderate.

Our culturally inherited language choices are so imbued with moralistic judgments that even when we seek to give "constructive" feedback, we are all too often met with defensiveness and countercriticism. We often perceive feedback as negative when we are being told that someone else doesn't like what we are doing. In part, this dynamic is explained by what we say and how we say it, but also it is explained by the acute sensitivity to criticism we have learned by being raised in cultures of blame.

In workplace evaluations, feedback often takes on a higher level of importance without a corresponding increase in its clarity or usefulness. Evaluations I've come across or heard about often rate people on a point scale in different arenas of work, such as punctuality, cooperativeness, motivation and attitude, and communication skills. The format of these evaluations imparts an appearance of impartiality to what is still a series of judgments. In addition, for the most part the categories are not really measurable.

The kind of feedback I prefer is generally tied to a specific observation, and is based on an assessment of whether needs have been met or not. This assessment is a kind of judgment—judging whether needs are met or unmet—however, in considering whether our needs have been met, we are not blaming or suggesting that anyone is deserving to be punished. When we give feedback, then, we let the other person know the observation (what they did or said that our feedback refers to), the needs met or unmet, and any requests we have. If we are on the receiving end of feedback, we can ask for the specific observation the feedback is based on, and guess (out loud or silently) the other person's needs. If the feedback is in the context of an evaluation report, each area of the evaluation can also be tied to specific observations and needs.

Practice Pause

Think of someone you give feedback to or receive feedback from. How might you clarify the feedback using the distinctions of NVC?

In my last years of being owner and manager of a law firm with twenty people, my law partner and I conducted annual reviews with each person in the firm. At that time, I was sharing my administrative assistant's time with a few other people in the firm, and we had a series of agreements about how work was to be shifted from one person to another depending on the priority of the work as opposed to the status of the requester. In other words, we had agreements about when other work was to be done before my work. Prior to the evaluations one year, several of our longtime and senior lawyer and paralegal staff came to my partner and me saying they wanted us to fire my assistant because of her attitude to doing work: by their assessment, she attempted to avoid doing work for others. They said she always put my work ahead of theirs even if theirs had a higher priority. I was inclined to acquiesce to their demands because of other interactions with her that had not been satisfying to me. Nonetheless, in the process of reflecting upon this step, I concluded that I was unwilling to take the drastic step of terminating someone's employment if I had not first satisfied myself that I had communicated to the person exactly what it is that I wanted them to do, and they had made clear that they were unwilling or unable to do it. In NVC terms, to terminate her without her having that prior set of communications would not have been in alignment with my values.

Consequently, my law partner and I decided that we would tell her, using observation language to the extent we understood it, what had stimulated distress in her coworkers, and be specific about what we would have liked her to do in those situations. I also told her the specific instances that were tied to my dissatisfaction. The review ended up being approximately two hours in length, much longer than our typical twenty- to thirty-minute review. My memory is that it was uncomfortable and emotional. Just as we were completing the review, my assistant said that though she did not find it enjoyable, it was the most valuable annual review she had ever experienced. We agreed that she would be on probation for three months and that she would have a review at the end of that time.

Within a month of the annual review, the people who had initially come to us wanting her dismissal returned one by one to tell us that their evaluation had changed completely, and that they wanted her to continue in her job. This was from people who, when I had told them I was unwilling to discharge her without having gone through a process that assured me that she understood what I wanted, had said that there was no way for her to change and that it was a waste of time to put her on probation.

I learned a lot from this experience. I was reinforced in my commitment to give observation- and need-based feedback to people as close in time as I am able. It also showed me how easy it is to develop an enemy image and, without testing the reality of that image, to live out of it and in doing so potentially harm someone. I also learned a bit about how much people crave specific feedback that informs them of what specific actions they can undertake to meet the needs of the person providing the evaluation, even if they're being told that their conduct is not satisfying.

The key preparation to communicating a negative evaluation to someone is to make sure your own needs for empathy are met and that you are clear as to what your intention is in communicating with the other person. Then, use observation language rather than judgment language when speaking about their conduct to make it as clear as you can what conduct you are referring to. Following the basic structure of the NVC training wheels sentence, you might then tell them the need of yours that is not met.

It seems to be much easier for people to hear negative evaluations when they are stated in observation language and followed by the need that isn't met, coupled with your request. Due to the training of our culture, they may still hear it as criticism; you cannot control how they will hear you and respond. However, you can be clear as to your intention and how you go about fulfilling that intention. As long as you are clear in your intention that you simply want them to understand that the conduct (expressed by you as an observation, free from judgment) is not meeting a need of yours, it may be easier for them to hear.

Your request is also key; it serves to help focus the person's mind on what you would like it to focus on and not on interpreting criticism when none is intended. A process request is often helpful when first stating the feedback: "Would you be willing to tell me how you feel hearing what I've said?" or "Would you be willing to tell me what you heard me say?" Once you are satisfied that you have been heard as you want, you can then make an action request, asking for the specific conduct you would like. A layer of difficulty is added when, for instance, we need to give feedback about something we don't like to a person whose decisions can adversely affect our continued employment. In such cases, additional self-empathy, and practice role-playing responses we anticipate would be challenging, may be necessary before we have the conversation. (See Example 17 below.)

Example 17

You leave a meeting with Magna feeling frustrated, thinking, "She always brings a bunch of new ideas; how are we supposed to implement all of these?" After doing self-empathy and silent empathy, you decide to give her feedback. Carefully preparing your statement beforehand, you first confirm her willingness to speak with you. Then you ask: "Magna, in our meeting when you brought in four new ideas for directions we can go in, I felt frustrated because I don't know how we could possibly do them all, as they all take a lot of time and energy. Are you laying them all out on the table because you are excited about them and want to share them with us?" Magna responds: "Yes, I just have so many ideas about what we can do! I don't mean for you to take them all as priorities!" You then make a request: "When you present new ideas like these, would you be willing to clarify when you are just sharing ideas for discussion and when you are presenting a new priority?"

When on the receiving end of a negative evaluation, it may help to remember whether the person giving it knows the distinctions of NVC. If you find yourself triggered by the feedback, practice self-empathy to reconnect with your own needs, or take a time-out if you need to do self-empathy away from the person. Then, use silent empathy to guess what needs the other person is trying to meet with their evaluation. You can then use your skills to respond to the person, translating what they said into Observations, Feelings, Needs, and Requests (if any), and checking your understanding of what was said with them. (See Example 18 below.)

Example 18

Magna wrote on your quarterly evaluation report, "You are too resistant to change." You do a lot of self-empathy about this statement, then decide to ask Magna for clarification. In your meeting, you ask, "Can you give me a specific example of when it seemed to you that I resisted change?" Magna says, "During our meeting about the Ferris project, when I said we needed to change a few things, you said they would take too long and seemed very disgruntled." You respond by saying, "So I can be clear about this, would you have liked me to have demonstrated to you my understanding of the changes you wanted and why you wanted them before I told you my concerns about being able to implement those changes?"

Sharing Common Work Areas

Another common workplace issue that provides opportunities to practice your new skills and get your needs met is the orderliness of shared areas. It seems that in every workplace, there are the neatniks and those who are not so neat. When the neatniks have had enough of dirty coffee mugs left in the sink, screaming signs are posted demanding that the not-neatniks clean up their dishes. (See Example 19 on page 99.)

If you see someone doing something you don't like in the work area, again, you can communicate to them in observation language, followed by the need of yours that is not met, and ending with your request. For example, after watching someone replace the empty coffee pot on the warmer after refilling their mug, you might say, "When I see you take the last of the coffee and not make a fresh pot, I feel frustrated because my needs for respect are not met. I'm wondering if you'd be willing to commit to making another pot of coffee when you take the last of it?" Their response may well be about time or some other reason for not making the coffee. In the law firm I helped found and manage, some of the lawyers would say their time was worth too much to be spent making coffee. If this is the type of response you receive, and you are comfortable with your skills, you might try to empathize with the person. If you are still uncomfortable or get triggered, you might instead use self-empathy and silent empathy.

Practice Pause

Choose a recurring issue in your workplace. How might you approach it differently using your new skills?

An alternative scenario here is that there may be an agreement in your workplace that a designated person is to make the coffee once it is empty. In that case, this example may instead be about requesting the person who empties the coffee dispenser to contact the designated coffee maker, or otherwise follow the agreements in your workplace.

If the person agrees to your request, then a further challenge comes when you see them do the same thing again, which leads to the question of how to handle broken agreements in the workplace.

Example 19

You notice that every time Harold has used the copy room, papers are left lying around and other supplies are not put away. After self-empathy for your frustration, you guess Harold is in a hurry when he leaves because he's feeling anxious about fulfilling his work commitments. When you run into him in the copy room, you say: "Harold, when paper and supplies are left out, I feel irritated, because I'd like to use the space without having to clean up first. Would you be willing to put things away when you are finished?"

Mediating Broken Agreements

In the workplace, a whole series of agreements are made that then generate pain for people when they are not kept: agreements about completing tasks and projects, starting and ending times for work and breaks, cleanliness of the office, and so on. The whole series of conversations around these broken agreements is a challenge of communication, from the initial conversation that establishes the agreement to the conversations following the perception that it has been broken.

Let's take an example from the manager's point of view, because, of course, this type of pain is not limited to the employees of the workplace. Perhaps, as a manager, you have an agreement with a person that they will arrive at work at a certain time, and then four out of five times this week they arrived fifteen minutes after the time they agreed to. What do you do?

When you notice that you are irritated or perhaps distressed as the result of having judgments about the other person, the first thing to do would be the enemy image process. This will help you clarify what needs of yours are not met by this situation, and as a result, you will probably be able to think more clearly about what your request of this person might be.

The first thing you might want to learn from this person is whether you share the same reality. One approach might be to say something like this: "My understanding was that you agreed you would arrive at work at 9:00 a.m., and I have observed this week that four out of five days you arrived fifteen minutes after that time. Would you tell me what has been going on for you?" By stating your observation in this way, you are trying to surface any assumptions and thus create a shared reality. By asking them to help you understand what was going on, you give them the opportunity to share with you, in colloquial language that you can then try to translate, the needs they were seeking to meet by their conduct. (See Example 20 on the next page.)

Practice Pause

Think of a recent time that someone broke an agreement with you. Use the enemy image process, then practice what you might say to them.

Compare this approach with a more typical managerial approach, which might be to say this: "Look, I just can't be having you show up late all the time. Either get here on time, or you'll be looking for a job." Notice that in the approach that seeks to create a shared reality through understanding each other's needs, the starting point is one of inquiry, not finality. When we inquire about the needs someone is seeking to meet by their conduct, we inquire about something that we can in fact have some leverage with. If you use the NVC words, but your intention is not one of caring—if you actually have the agenda of "it's my way or the highway"—the words will not matter; your underlying intention will likely come across. Thus, it is important to do the enemy image process or in some way get your needs for empathy met first.

Once you understand what needs the other person was seeking to meet, you can then express to them what needs of yours are not met by their arriving later than agreed. If both parties understand the needs, then the inquiry turns to strategies that meet everyone's needs. This, in my own experience and from reports of others, is a much more satisfying route than the "typical" managerial response.

Example 20

Though Harold has agreed to put things away in the copy room, you notice that he leaves them out again the next few times he uses the room. You ask him: "Harold, my understanding was that you agreed to put things away when you were finished with them. Did you have a different understanding?" He says, "Well, I figured at the end of the week would be fine." You respond with, "Are you wanting to get back to work without taking the time to clean up?"

"Yeah, I don't see what the big deal is."

You decide to try expression again: "When I come in and see stuff lying out on the tables, I'm frustrated because it's difficult to use the table without clearing it first, and then I'm not as effective in my work. I'd really like some support and consideration around the space being left neat. Would you be willing to spend some time right now looking at how we might create a system in here that will work for us both?"

Answering Email

Many of us receive more email daily than we enjoy, and here again is an opportunity to develop fluency and ease with Nonviolent Communication distinctions. The first place to practice is using self-empathy when you feel overwhelmed upon opening your in-box to find more new messages than you want to deal with! Taking a deep breath and connecting with your feelings and needs before diving into organizing, reading, and answering the messages may help the process proceed more smoothly.

Practice Pause

What is your relationship with email? How might NVC shift that relationship?

I still use email to practice integrating NVC into my life, but early on it was particularly helpful. There are really two parts to using email as a practice to gain more fluency—reading the email and responding to it. When reading the email, I would (and still do) try to guess the needs behind the words used in the email, and thus practice silent empathy.

To respond, I often wrote emails in a classic NVC style, using the training wheels sentence; then I typically edited them to be more colloquial. Doing this helped me structure my responses and get clear about what I wanted to say. It was a form of empathy to express myself initially in the form "When I read this in your email, I feel . . . , because I need . . . Would you be willing to . . . ?" This also showed me how easy it was to lose track of the basic NVC distinctions. When I tried to simply write colloquially, I found I would embed judgments and confuse needs and strategies. (See Example 21 on facing page.)

If I receive an email that I interpret is expressing a lot of pain, I may decide that I'm not going to be able to effectively empathize using email; it has not been, for me, a forum that has been conducive to giving empathy. My strategy is to respond to such emails with some attempt at connection and then a request that we set up a telephone call or face-to-face meeting. I might write something like this: "I'd really like to understand better what you're getting at in your email; however, I'm not at all confident that I'll be able to do that by email. So, would you be willing to schedule a telephone call? Here are the times that I'm available . . . "

Example 21

You receive an email addressed to both you and Harold from Karen. It says: "Would one of you give me some feedback on the attached document? Thanks!"

You first write a response following classic NVC: "Karen, when I read your email, I feel annoyed because I need clarity around who you want feedback from and what feedback you want. Would you be willing to direct your message to one person and state specifically what feedback you are looking for?" Then you rewrite it: "Karen, would you be willing to clarify your email? I'd like to know who you actually want feedback from and what kind of feedback. Would you be more specific? Thanks!"

Transforming the End of Employment

Whether you are leaving a job or asking someone else to leave, the conversations that are part of ending employment are typically fraught with stressful emotions. When we face the possibility of losing a job or leaving one that has been unsatisfying, we often become uncertain how we will meet our needs for security and contribution. As managers, we may be reluctant to deal with all that is stimulated in ourselves and others when we ask someone to leave. To protect ourselves from dealing with these emotions, we may opt to avoid engaging with the issues. This section suggests a way of looking at the ending of employment as a series of conversations and reviews suggestions made in this book that can help you navigate your way through the process.

Typically, employment problems are solved with what I would call the use of force. I consider something to be "force" whenever someone acts unilaterally and does not include the other person's needs in their considerations. If as an employee, I quit without any conversations that attempt to work out the situation and leave without valuing my own and my manager's needs equally, or attempting to maintain any kind of connection, then I have used force. Similarly, as a manager, I use force if I fire someone without communicating my expectations and trying to make requests and agreements based on mutual needs. If I value acting with integrity, maintaining connection with people, and caring for others' needs—with the understanding that my own needs are best met when theirs are met—then the use of force will not be my preferred solution.

I think of the decision to end employment as a process that consists of a series of communications occurring both before and after the actual termination. The first series of conversations lead up to the one in which the end of employment is communicated. Perhaps the manager or employee is unhappy with some aspect of the situation, or perhaps changed circumstances mean the employee cannot continue in the position in the same manner. Many conversations may take place in which both parties attempt to work out a suitable agreement, and NVC is particularly useful for exploring the options available in these cases. When at least one of the parties is able to repeatedly clarify their own needs, guess the other person's needs, and make requests that attempt to meet all of those needs, such connection can lead either to transforming the job or to ending employment in a more satisfying way to all parties than unilateral action.

After employment has ended, a series of communications often continue afterward, wrapping up aspects of the work, turning things over to another employee, or finalizing provisions of the termination agreement. There are, of course, exceptions in which only limited conversations may occur—such as in the case of budget cuts leading to layoffs. However, even in these cases, some communication inevitably takes place in the process.

The key to moving through this often-stressful process is to continuously reconnect with yourself. Using NVC for self-care purposes can help you not only manage the distress the situation may stimulate, no matter your role, but also find strategies more likely to create what you want. For example, all of the employment-ending situations I have been involved in (and I have been on both sides more than once) have been replete with enemy images on both sides. I had my share of judgments about the others involved, and I am confident they also had enemy images of me (see "Recognizing Enemy Images"). When I was able to do my own enemy image work as part of my self-care and preparation, I was subsequently able to relate to the situation in a way I much preferred. Connecting with the needs behind my judgmental thoughts and then connecting with what I thought might be going on with the other person effectively shifted how I perceived my reality and therefore how I acted in the situation.

In addition to using NVC for self-care, you can use the concepts we have discussed throughout this book to approach the employment-ending process as a series of difficult conversations. Each conversation can be approached as a learning opportunity, utilizing what we discussed in this chapter in the section on "Handling Difficult Conversations." You can prepare and practice for a conversation using the enemy image process (see "The Enemy Image Process" in this chapter). Afterward, you can take some time to reflect on how it went, celebrating and mourning the ways that a conversation did or did not meet your needs (see "Celebrating and Mourning in NVC" in Chapter 3). This process can then help you consider your next step. Since giving and receiving feedback, whether in formal evaluations or informal conversations, is commonly a prelude to ending employment, you might also review "Giving Feedback and Evaluations" in this chapter. Other sections in this chapter, such as "Navigating Power Differentials," may also prove helpful depending on your situation.

I like to think of the whole process as a mediation of my own needs and the needs of the others involved. I encourage you to see each conversation as an opportunity to (1) clarify the needs you want to be met in the situation, (2) clarify the needs of the other person or persons involved, and (3) make requests intended to lead to agreements that meet everyone's needs. Whether you are leaving a position or asking someone else to leave, I encourage you to appreciate and utilize the power you have to change your world through how you talk about it with others and yourself.

Now, I'm sure we can all think of situations in which the kind of communication I'm talking about has not helped. Perhaps someone was so stimulated or in pain about something that they were not able to have a conversation about what needed to change. Perhaps you tried to communicate your needs and make requests and agreements, and these have not resulted in the kind of behavioral change that meets your needs. In these types of situations, I do find myself willing to use force—that is, to act unilaterally without taking into account the other person's needs. I call this "the protective use of force," a phrase borrowed from Marshall Rosenberg.

Here is a simple example of what I mean by *protective use of force*: If you see a two-year-old running into the street, and a car is coming, you don't call to get the child's attention or make a guess as to what needs the child is attempting to meet by running into the street. No! You act to protect. You scoop up the child to safety. To me the key to the protective use of force is to take action without anger, without seeking to punish the child or to induce shame or guilt. In other words, the idea is to take your unilateral action with a sense of compassion both for yourself and for the other person.

To translate this into the workplace, then, let's say you are in a situation where you are responsible for someone's continuing employment. This person has consistently acted in ways that are not meeting your needs, and you are confident they understand that their actions are not meeting your needs. Perhaps they make sexually explicit comments to coworkers, or they have on enumerated occasions not been there when they said they would be (yet they are in a position where you need predictability). You have tried to talk to this person, clarifying your own needs and guessing theirs. You have made requests and agreements, and have seen no change in response. You might feel that you have exhausted all of the options you know for handling the situation in a way that will meet both your and the other person's needs.

Or, let's say you are an employee in a situation where going to work has become increasingly painful. Perhaps the work environment has changed due to others acting in ways that don't meet your needs. You have communicated with those involved and have found that it has not created the kind of connection you would like. You know of no other way to get your needs met.

These are the types of situations in which I become willing to act unilaterally, calling on my understanding of the protective use of force. If I have sought to care about and include the needs of the other person, attempted to get clear about my needs, communicated my needs and made requests, and formulated and revisited agreements, then at some point I become unwilling to continue trying to engage with the other person in a communication process. The question becomes "With what attitude do I take action?" If I want to exercise the protective use of force, then to the best of my ability, I take action without anger, and without any attempt to punish the other person or induce feelings of shame, guilt, blame, or depression. I do whatever inner work is necessary for me to act with some sense of compassion for myself and for the other person. Without compassion, I have only the typical method of resolving issues in the workplace: using force over another person.

I use this concept of the protective use of force to personally assess my own conduct, to see whether I am acting consistently with my values. This is not in any way an externally verifiable standard. In other words, though I may feel certain I have exhausted my options in a situation, I recognize that someone with more skill or knowledge might find further options to try. In fact, I find that when I question myself about a situation some time after the fact, I generally find myself mourning possibilities I see now that I did not see then. I then learn from my mourning process so that if I meet a similar situation again, I will have this knowledge to call upon. As long as I am honest with myself and accept that I am doing the best I can in a given situation, the concept of the protective use of force helps me take responsibility for my actions and focus my mind on how to take those actions out of compassion. This focus becomes a powerful motivating force for me; it's a way of measuring my integrity.

Using NVC skills and concepts does not determine a particular outcome, of course. These skills are not recipes that guarantee you will keep a job or relieve you of the difficulty of firing an employee. Sometimes terminating employment is in the best interests of everyone involved, and sometimes other solutions are found. However, as you use the skills and processes offered in this book and gain skill with them, your ability to stay connected with yourself and others, even through the difficulties involved in ending employment, will increase. The outcomes that emerge are more likely to be ones that satisfy your needs and values.

Chapter 7

Workplace Communication Tips

INTRODUCTION

When *Words That Work in Business* was originally published, the author and publishers created a set of fifty-two weekly tips based on the content of the book. The idea behind the tips was to break down the information in the book to bite-size pieces and combine them with a Mindful Practice to help people actually integrate the information into their lives. After all, we all know how easy it is to read a book, know how helpful the knowledge could be, and then fall short on implementing a process to practice and put the information to use! The following tips were intended to create such a structure for you.

If that structure feels helpful for you, you can still sign up to receive these as a weekly email series; just go to www.nonviolentcommunication. com/workplace_tips/wpc_index.htm and input your email address.

The fifty-two tips series is also included in this section for you to use as makes most sense for you in your learning process. You might create your own weekly plan of coming back to the book to pick another tip to practice and use during the following days. Or perhaps you simply pick up the book periodically when you're ready for a new practice and find another tip that resonates with you based on what is going on at work.

Think of these as reminders of what you've learned and quick simple ways to practice so that you can easily and effectively use the skills in the book in your workplace. Notice that each time you use them you will be in the learning cycle described in Chapter 3: trying something out, reflecting on how it went based on needs, and choosing what to try next. In this way, you will constantly be on a growth trajectory and the skills will become more and more your own.

"As you identify . . . the needs that were and were not met by your actions, . . . space opens within us to act differently in the future." (Page 110)

TIP #1: TAKING THE FIRST STEP

Have you ever found yourself in a repeat pattern of dissatisfaction in your work relationships? Do you long for improved productivity or synergy with your team, or in the level of support or respect you receive from your boss or coworkers?

Considering that most of us spend a third of our day working, commuting, or thinking about work or commuting, why wouldn't we want these things?

The first step is to take a look at yourself—recognizing your own habitual thinking and behavior that may be keeping you from the workplace experience you want. Even if you change jobs altogether, these habitual patterns are likely to surface again and again.

Learning to connect with your behavior at the level of needs is a way to step out of your habitual ways of reacting. As you identify, time and time again, the needs that were and were not met by your actions, particularly in situations where you reacted habitually, space opens within you to act differently in the future.

For example, let's say you react habitually to a coworker's remark. Next time this happens, instead of looking outward (with blame or judgment of your coworker or a search through the want ads), take a look at yourself.

You might discover your reaction was not in harmony with your values. You might inquire into the need you were seeking to meet by your reaction—such as respect, acknowledgment, or support—and alternately what need was not met when you responded the way you did. The natural result of this inquiry is the question, "How might I do it differently the next time to better meet my needs?"

Mindful Practice

This week, pause to recognize one habitual reaction you have with a coworker, boss, or customer. Ask yourself if this reaction is in harmony with your values. What needs were met or not met by this reaction?

"By being connected with our own needs, our intention is clarified moment by moment." (Page 7)

TIP #2: USE YOUR TRAINING WHEELS

Are you ambitious? Have you found yourself impatient to fully incorporate your new NVC skills into your workplace communication so you can start seeing results?

Learning to ingrain the basic distinctions of NVC at a deep level requires a reprogramming of your thinking so you can act out of an intention that is in better alignment with your values. Simply put, it takes time and practice.

Using what is called the NVC training wheels sentence helps you begin to ingrain the four basic distinctions of NVC, each of which is imbedded in the training wheels sentence.

Here are the four basic distinctions of NVC and the Training Wheels Sentence:

1. Observations: "When I hear . . .,"
2. Feelings: "I feel . . .,"
3. Needs: "Because I need . . ."
4. Requests: "Would you be willing to . . .?

People who skip this stage tend to take longer to really embody the perspective-altering potential of NVC, if they ever do. Practicing the training wheels sentence is the most effective way to get these basic distinctions at a deep level.

Instead of skipping past the training wheels, embrace them as a critical and necessary part of reaching the future results you seek.

Mindful Practice

This week, keep the training wheels sentence at hand: "When I hear/see . . . I feel . . . because I need . . . Would you be willing to . . .?" Use it at least once a day to reflect on an interaction you had. Notice how it connects you to the four distinctions of NVC.

"There is almost nothing a person can say or do that cannot be responded to either with empathy or with some form of self-connected expression." (Page 9)

TIP #3: WHICH COMES FIRST, THE CHICKEN OR THE EGG?

Do you find you have trepidation about using NVC at work? Are you fearful that coworkers will wonder why you're talking so strangely? Your fear may become a chicken-or-the-egg challenge where you ask, "How do I get the skills if I'm afraid to use them? Yet, how do I use them safely without having the skills?"

A powerful way to develop NVC skills in the workplace is through silent practice. You can practice the inner work of NVC without anyone knowing.

One powerful method of silent practice is called "Awareness of Blocking Connection." The two steps of this practice help us recognize the many ways our communication itself can block connection.

Silently, take these steps:

1. Notice the times when you feel less than connected while speaking with a coworker or boss.
2. When you notice you are not feeling as connected as you would like, determine whether either of you are doing any of the following: defending a position, explaining, moralistically judging, diagnosing others, blaming, seeking to punish, or "needing" to be right. Any internal sense of wanting the other to feel guilt or shame also tends to generate disconnection.

Recognizing and becoming conscious and aware of these barriers to connection is a powerful initial step in the NVC learning process.

Mindful Practice

This week, pause to silently reflect on a conversation or encounter at work that didn't go well. Ask yourself if you experienced thinking that may have blocked your ability to stay compassionate.

> **"Knowing before you start speaking what need you're trying to get met and what your request is has a couple of benefits."** (Page 49)

TIP #4: DO YOU KNOW YOUR TRIGGERS?

The workplace can be a feeding ground for conflict. The difference between a workplace that leaves you triggered and reactive and one that stimulates outstanding relationships and productivity starts with knowing your triggers.

A trigger can be word, a behavior, or anything that stirs up negative feelings. Instead of reacting to the trigger with anger, words, or behavior you might regret, you can use the trigger as an opportunity to recognize what needs of yours are not being met.

Without awareness, a trigger leads you into a habitual reaction. Whatever your reactive pattern is—whether anger, judgment, or stewing quietly—chances are it isn't ultimately meeting your needs.

Self-empathy is an effective tool to intervene at the moment you're triggered so you can choose to respond differently. If an interaction just happened, you can use self-empathy and the training wheels sentence to connect to your feelings and needs:

"When I hear/see . . ., I feel . . ., because I need . . ."

Mindful Practice

This week, try to recognize as many of your triggers as possible. Create a running list describing the behavior, language, or experience that left you triggered, building a new awareness of their connection to habitual responses.

"When we are in pain and our thoughts are awhirl, we are not able to empathize with others until our need for empathy has been sufficiently met." (Page 16)

TIP #5: WE NEED TO TALK ABOUT IT <u>NOW</u>!

In the interest of efficiency, productivity, and teamwork, do you ever force yourself to talk through a conflict or encounter with a colleague before you're ready? You might think talking it through is the best way to defuse your anger or frustration and ultimately get back to work.

Unfortunately, taking this route may only lead to further disconnection and frustration—for both of you.

Before you dive in to "talk it out" with your coworker or boss, take a few minutes to give yourself empathy and connect to your feelings and needs.

If you are anticipating a difficult conversation with someone, a tough meeting, or a challenging interaction, practice self-empathy beforehand with these steps:

1. Observation: Identify what was actually said or done without judgment.
2. Feelings: Identify how you feel about it, without evaluation.
3. Needs: Identify what need was met or not met by the words or actions, without blame.

As you prepare for the interaction with self-empathy, notice any changes in your thought process and in how you feel. How has this process shifted your intention as you go into the conversation?

Mindful Practice

This week, give yourself permission to pause—employing the steps of self-empathy—before entering a difficult conversation, meeting, or encounter with a colleague or customer. Continue the practice until you recognize a shift in your intention away from judgment, blame, or "being right."

"Even if you did no other practice, consistently meeting your need for empathy would be life-changing in and of itself." (Page 16)

TIP #6: WHAT'S GOING ON FOR YOU?

Tip #5 explored the value of using self-empathy to help you approach a difficult conversation from an intention of connection, rather than defensiveness, anger, or pain.

After you've given yourself adequate empathy, your attention and focus will likely turn to the other person, and the question that typically arises is some version of "What is going on with them?"

If you ask this question before having met your own need for empathy, your mind will typically jump to analyzing the other person's "wrongness" with thoughts like "None of this would have happened if he hadn't been such a jerk." When you are full of empathy, however, the question becomes "Which needs of theirs are they seeking to meet?"

You can ask this question safely by using silent empathy, which works the same as self-empathy except that you are internally inquiring about another person instead of yourself. You're guessing what is going on with the other person, what needs they are trying to meet with their action or behavior.

With these two steps completed—self-empathy and silent empathy—you'll find your demeanor, your body language, your presence, and your intention may have shifted into a space of compassion or at least more understanding and openness. From this space, you are much more likely to meet your needs as well as those of the other person.

Mindful Practice

This week, practice the tools of self-empathy and silent empathy to prepare for a difficult conversation or encounter. Pay close attention to shifts you experience in how you feel, your body language, and your self-talk as you do so.

"NVC is not about changing the way you talk; it's about changing the way you think and the way you view the world." (Page 168)

TIP #7: PRACTICE, PRACTICE, PRACTICE

You don't need to wait until you're triggered, upset, or angry to practice self-empathy or silent empathy. The more you practice, the more natural and automatic empathy will feel, so take advantage of the many opportunities that the workplace offers:

1. Meetings: Use silent empathy to translate your coworker's comments into feelings and needs.
2. Your commute: If you find yourself triggered on your morning or evening commute, take a deep breath. Use self-empathy to connect to your feelings and needs. Use silent empathy to

connect to the needs of your fellow commuters, with emphasis on those drivers who may have just triggered you.

3. Email: Before shooting off a reactive email to a colleague, write a practice email using your NVC self-empathy training wheels—noting your own observations, feelings, and needs in response to your colleague's behavior. Now, write another practice email using silent empathy, guessing what needs were met for your colleague by their behavior. Be sure to end with a request, even something like "Is that true for you?" or "did I get it?"

Mindful Practice

This week, commit to practice silent empathy and self-empathy interchangeably, noticing any shifts you experience in your body language, physical presence, and intention as a result.

"A person will react to me differently because of my body language, the words I use, and how I use them." (Page 19)

TIP #8: THE BLAME GAME

We've all played the blame game at work, that game of who is at fault—you or someone else—for what isn't right about a situation. It's easy to play the blame game because it is embedded in our language:

- "He's not at fault."
- "She didn't have any other choice."
- "So what else could they have done?"
- "I had to do it."

The feelings associated with blaming and punishing are anger, depression, shame, and guilt. Not surprisingly, it can be very difficult to meet your needs when you're assessing blame, avoiding punishment, and alternately feeling angry, depressed, ashamed, or guilty.

How often do you find yourself in this blame game cycle at work?

Mindful Practice

This week, become more aware of those moments when you find yourself playing the blame game. Recognize in the moment how this cycle limits your choices, particularly choices that could result in much more positive outcomes for everyone.

"Celebration . . . is the heart of gratitude—feeling grateful for what you and others have done to create the world more to your liking." (Page 22)

TIP #9: A JOB WELL DONE

Sometimes we get so caught up in naming behaviors that "need improvement" that we forget to celebrate a job well done. Even seemingly simple accomplishments like a conversation, a meeting, or a team interaction that went especially well are worth celebrating.

Unfortunately, sometimes our celebration stops with a simple phrase like "thank you" or "good job," neither of which provide any concrete understanding of what is being celebrated.

Rather than just celebrate the accomplishment with these empty phrases, NVC offers a framework to engage in a more meaningful celebration, right at the level of needs.

Let's say you're celebrating an encounter you had with an angry customer, and you're especially satisfied with your ability to defuse the customer using empathy. As you recall this interaction, ask yourself, "How do I feel and which of my needs are met as a result of what I did?"

You might answer: "I feel satisfied and confident because the customer expressed she liked how I listened to her and that she believed I care about her situation. My needs for contribution and integrity were met with this conversation."

What recent interaction or accomplishment do you want to celebrate?

Mindful Practice

This week identify something you want to celebrate at the level of needs. Use the steps described above to communicate this celebration to yourself or others. Notice any change you experience as a result of using a needs-based celebration instead of a simple "good job."

"When I connect with the need that was not met, I know I've connected with the need I want to be met, and my mind then looks for strategies to meet it." (Page 22)

TIP #10: THIS PERSON "NEEDS IMPROVEMENT"

Have you ever received feedback from a coworker or boss that sounded something like:

- "He's difficult to get along with."
- "She isn't a team player."
- "No one likes to work with him because he's a poor communicator."

- "You're not pulling your weight around here."

It's no surprise that feedback like this typically doesn't lead to improved behavior; rather it often just leaves you feeling angry, depressed, ashamed, or guilty.

If you've had an interaction or encounter at work that didn't go the way you'd like, don't get caught up in similar judgments of yourself.

Instead, mourn the experience using self-empathy. Doing so helps you shift away from unproductive self-judgment back into the learning cycle.

You can practice mourning without your coworker present, either in your head or with the support of a friend. Start the minute you're aware that you didn't enjoy an interaction, observing your reaction, the feelings your reaction stirred up in you, and the needs that were not met.

If you long to free yourself from labels and judgments in the workplace, your first step is to stop judging yourself.

Mindful Practice

This week, become more aware of the moments when you are burdened by self-judgment or the judgment of a coworker because of an interaction you had. Become curious how you could move beyond this judgment through the process of mourning.

> **"In the beginning of learning to incorporate a new skill, it is crucial to find ways to remind ourselves that it is an option."** (Page 27)

TIP #11: PUT IT IN WRITING

When we get caught up in our day-to-day lives, it is easy to forget that we wanted to incorporate NVC.

Making a commitment to daily practice can remind you that these skills are available and that you are interested in trying them out. Consider writing your commitment down and placing it near your desk as a reminder. It can also be helpful to have another person—such as a practice partner—involved in your commitment for accountability and extra support.

One easy method to commit to daily practice is through daily mourning and celebration with your partner, either live, by phone, or even by email. However small or seemingly insignificant, this daily practice helps build your awareness of the four NVC distinctions while also building your awareness of your own behavior.

On your own, or with your practice partner, express one thing you'd like to mourn—observing the experience without judgment, expressing what you felt, and what needs were not met. Then, express one thing you'd like to celebrate using the same process, yet noting what needs were met.

Mindful Practice

This week, put your commitment to daily practice on paper and place it in a prominent location. If you feel inspired to do so, find a practice partner as well.

> **"The fundamental benefit of my daily practice has been the shift out of the blame and punishment paradigm and into the learning paradigm."** (Page 28)

TIP #12: "YOU'RE JUST RUDE . . ."

"If I'm not connected with myself, and I'm finding the memory of something that happened the day before painful, I am typically in a blame and punishment paradigm" (page 28).

This means you're either blaming somebody else or yourself for what was or was not done. This paradigm is common in the workplace and it stems from a focus on what we do not like instead of what we would like.

For instance, if a coworker is short with me in a meeting I might respond with, "This person is rude," and nothing transforms. Simply telling yourself to stop blaming or judging isn't enough.

Instead, use the process of mourning and state an observation: "This person is acting in a way I don't enjoy, that doesn't meet my need for respect." Now you have owned the experience and your mind has shifted to something it can transform, your need for respect.

Using silent empathy in the moment can prove an important factor to quickly transform the blame and judgment paradigm. It can also be a good antidote to burnout.

Mindful Practice

In the coming week, recognize an encounter that led you into blame or judgment thinking. Recall the situation and use the process of mourning to connect to your feelings and needs. Become curious how this step shifts you away from blame thinking.

> **"If I'm not connected to myself, and I'm finding the memory of something that happened the day before painful, I am typically in a blame and punishment paradigm."** (Page 28)

TIP #13: BUILD YOUR EMOTIONAL VOCABULARY

Have you ever struggled to accurately name your feelings beyond simple words like good, bad, sad, or angry? If so, you're certainly not alone.

The workplace has historically been a space where feelings and needs had no merit, and often have been perceived as a threat to productivity. Workers are expected to remain rational, putting a cap on their feelings and needs.

Checking in with our feelings and needs meets our need for empathy. In so doing we are often far more productive than we could be when our needs are left unacknowledged.

Building your vocabulary of feelings and needs can have a profound effect on your awareness of them in the moment. Keep your list of feelings and needs on hand. At the moment you're unclear what you're feeling or needing, use this "cheat sheet" to help.

Mindful Practice

This week, keep your list of feelings and needs (Appendixes B and D) handy. Use it throughout your day to name a feeling or need you struggle to identify on your own. Start to notice how your improved vocabulary also helps you more accurately guess the feelings and needs of those around you.

> **"The inner work of NVC can be done without anyone knowing."** (Page 9)

TIP #14: GO AHEAD, PUT YOURSELF OUT THERE

The key to moving through the learning curve of Nonviolent Communication in the workplace is practice. There are many opportunities throughout your day to practice your communication skills silently—from the morning or evening commute, to your lunch hour, to down time as you walk between meetings.

Making a committed effort to use those opportunities will help you build confidence and competence in your new vocabulary, with no real risk.

It will also go far in shifting your thinking so empathy more naturally becomes your immediate response, regardless of the situation.

How could you "put yourself out there"? Can you think of some opportunities at work where you'll likely be triggered and you can safely practice your silent empathy or self-empathy skills?

Mindful Practice

This week, identify at least one opportunity each day where you can "put yourself out there" and practice NVC using self-empathy or silent empathy.

> **"The key to moving through the learning curve
> and gaining competence is practice."** (Page 31)

TIP #15: "WHY ARE YOU TALKING SO WEIRD?"

As you learn and use a new way of communicating, people who know you are likely to take notice, perhaps wondering what motivated the shift. They might even ask, "Why are you talking like that?" The curiosity—or even the judgment—of those around you might be enough to send you cowering in self-conscious embarrassment.

Practicing our NVC skills out loud is an essential part of the learning process and finding the "right" practice partner is key to practicing safely and confidently. The best place to find a practice partner is either in your outermost or innermost circle.

- Innermost circle: your intimate relationships with partners, family members, or even close colleagues who are the most familiar with you.
- Outermost circle: people you interact with who don't know you and whom you aren't necessarily likely to stay in contact with, such as taxi drivers, salespeople, or others you interact with in the course of daily life.

If you choose a practice partner in your innermost circle, it's important to get their buy in first so you know you have permission to stumble without judgment.

You can even create a verbal agreement with them such as: "I am interested in something called Nonviolent Communication, and I'm going to start trying to use it more, so I'm going to be saying some things in ways that are a little different from before. If at any time you feel uncomfortable or don't like what I'm saying, I'd really like to hear it right away, and for us to deal with it."

This type of agreement tends to build a safe place for you to practice without fear of criticism and openness on your partner's end to provide helpful feedback in the moment.

Mindful Practice

In the week ahead, think about someone in your innermost circle you might make a practice agreement with. Practice how you might phrase this request.

"In most situations, I will increase the likelihood of getting what I want if I ask for it." (Page 38)

TIP #16: "PERMISSION TO FALTER, PLEASE . . ."

Last week's tip talked about your options for practicing NVC with someone in your innermost circle—someone among your intimate relationships who knows you very well. The tip also emphasized the importance of creating an agreement with your practice partner to ensure their buy-in.

Let's say you practice at home around your family using the training wheels sentence. Without a connection to your intention and commitment to learning, you can appear disingenuous because your speech sounds stifled and forced, or your "old self" and "new self" are in conflict.

One type of practice agreement that works well is called an awareness agreement. Here, your partner agrees to support you in continually clarifying the key distinctions within the four-part NVC process:

1. Observations vs. judgments;
2. Feelings vs. evaluations masquerading as feelings;

3. Needs vs. strategies to meet my needs; and

4. Requests versus demands.

For instance, as you share how your workday went, your partner can remind you to make these distinctions in your description.

Mindful Practice

Who in your innermost circle might you make an awareness agreement with? Think about how you might phrase that agreement, and then try it out with them this week.

"Having the presence of mind to request help and make an agreement around an unconscious behavior helped me become aware of that behavior." (Page 43)

TIP #17: "HOLD ME ACCOUNTABLE, PLEASE!"

A second type of practice agreement that works well is called an accountability agreement.

These agreements are based on our knowledge that while we are attempting to incorporate a new set of values and skills into our lives, the reality is that we will likely be triggered in heated moments to react out of our habitual patterns. We make accountability agreements with people to empower them to point out to us when they see us acting in a way that's out of alignment with how we've stated we want to act.

If this type of agreement will work best for your learning needs, put one in writing with your practice partner.

Be specific about the response you'd like to hear from your practice partner as these moments arise. Think about a question they could ask or response they could give that is least likely to trigger you even more (for example, instead of "That's a judgment!" perhaps they ask, "Is that an observation or a judgment?"). Put it in writing. And be willing to modify the agreement as you gain more experience with it. Remember, you have the agreement to aid your learning and not as a test of whether you will keep it as originally conceived.

Mindful Practice

Think about a behavior you're trying to change. Who in your life could you make an accountability agreement with to help you change it? What is the specific question or response you'd like to hear from them?

> **"Without practice, it is unlikely that your intention to connect and communicate with others will ever be realized."** (Page 44)

TIP #18: WHAT IS YOUR INTENTION?

Learning new communication skills can empower you with new knowledge and hope for a more positive interaction with coworkers in the future.

In some cases, we can become so excited by the possibility of a more positive interaction that we begin to think of NVC as the only tool to get us there. We begin to push these news skills onto our coworkers, disconnecting from the original intention and turning to judgment: "If my coworkers would just 'do it right,' we wouldn't have this conflict!"

As you practice your NVC skills, it's important to ground yourself in your intention. Otherwise you run the risk of using your new skills from a space of defense or offense, a place of judgment and superiority, rather than from your desire to support improved connection for all.

In addition to creating practice agreements, clarify your intention of learning and using NVC on paper as well. What is your hope in acquiring new skills and developing a more compassionate consciousness?

Mindful Practice

This week, think through your intention of learning and using NVC skills in the workplace. Write your intention on paper so you can continue to reconnect to this intention as you practice.

"Sometimes, in the workplace, the best we are able to do may be to remove ourselves from the situation in order to give ourselves empathy and reconnect with our needs." (Page 44)

TIP #19: TAKING THE TIME YOU NEED

When we're not in the space of compassionate intention and we're triggered, sometimes removing ourselves from the situation for a few minutes is the best solution. However, how we remove ourselves will help prevent triggering others in turn when we give ourselves that space.

For instance, if you find yourself triggered during a conversation with a coworker, ask for a short break, but be clear about this request and own it. Clarify that your intention is to take a few minutes to reconnect and regroup, and that you want to come back later to re-engage in the conversation.

You can also say something like "I'm going to the bathroom," when you anticipate that your desire to regroup won't be well received, or it isn't appropriate to communicate (such as in a meeting).

By taking this "time-out" you're actually taking a "time in" to give yourself empathy and reconnect to your intention to make a compassionate connection.

Mindful Practice

This week, find ways to remind yourself to take a "time in" as you need it. Breathe and use silent and/or self-empathy to reconnect with your feelings and needs.

"Some people fear the vulnerability they think they will experience if they ask for what they really want." (Page 47)

TIP #20: IF YOU WANT IT, ASK FOR IT

Self-editing refers to conversations we have in our head when we are thinking about what we want that run something like this: "Well, I really want him to let me know ahead of time when he is going to spring a completely new project on me so I can prepare for it. But he has always done this and he won't change, and even if he does, I still will have to fit it in to everything else I'm already doing, so why bother asking for it?"

In other words, you think your needs are not going to get met, and you think asking might undermine your relationship, so you don't even ask.

When you self-edit, you begin to realize that you're operating out of some beliefs about the other person or the situation, or perhaps even yourself. For instance, maybe your belief is "He doesn't care what I think" or "He'll just hear my request as a criticism" or "She'll ultimately do whatever she wants anyway."

With this awareness, take a look at these beliefs and find the need behind them. Then ask yourself if you want to test the belief by making an actual request of your coworker.

Mindful Practice

This week, notice if you are self-editing to talk yourself out of making a clear request. Try to uncover the beliefs behind the self-editing, connecting to the need behind them.

"The clearer I get, the clearer my request gets, and the clearer the other person can be about their own response to it." (Page 48)

TIP #21: DREAMS ARE VAGUE, REQUESTS ARE CLEAR

Do you ever get frustrated at work because a coworker didn't follow through on what you'd asked them to do?

In many situations, while you thought your request was clear, upon deeper analysis you might realize you haven't asked for anything at all.

A common pattern that hinders our ability to make clear requests is that we don't recognize the difference between a broad, general dream for something different or better, and a specific, doable, concrete future action one can take to support us in fulfilling that dream.

When you communicate a dream as a request, the communication is open to broad interpretation. Your coworker might hear your dream as just that and do nothing in response. Another coworker might hear it as a request and take a specific action, but likely not the action you had in mind. And your response to both might be one of judgment, "No one here takes me seriously" or "This team is so uncooperative!"

Differentiating between a vague dream and a clear, actionable request could be the difference between continued frustration and actually getting what you want.

Mindful Practice

This week, notice how you state your requests. Are they actionable? Or are they more a general "dream"? How could you translate this dream into a clear request?

"You cannot control how your communication will be received; you can only control your intention and your actions—what you say and do." (Pages 50–51)

TIP #22: ANATOMY OF A CLEAR REQUEST

The previous tip talked about differentiating between a vague "dream" of a future you desire and a request that could help fulfill this dream.

Clear requests are:

- Doable
- Present tense
- Stated in action language

The basic distinction inherent in Nonviolent Communication requests is that they are not demands, meaning there is no accompanying threat of physical or emotional force or negative consequences if the request is not agreed to.

But even when your request meets these parameters, the real distinction between a request and a demand is in your intention. You might actually use the same exact words to make a request or a demand. Yet if you are asking someone out of "demand energy," then you are not making a request, regardless of the words you use.

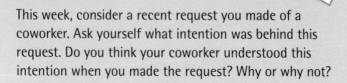

Mindful Practice

This week, consider a recent request you made of a coworker. Ask yourself what intention was behind this request. Do you think your coworker understood this intention when you made the request? Why or why not?

"When you are clear about your request, you usually find you can state it in a few words." (Page 49)

TIP #23: "I CAN'T DO THAT!"

Tip #22 described the first component of a clear request as one that is "doable." To make a request *doable* seems simple enough, until we realize how often our requests are not doable.

A boss saying to a subordinate, "You need to not take things so personally!" may sound on the surface like a reasonable request, but it is not doable. This request leaves out a crucial piece of information—what specific conduct does the boss anticipate would meet his need?

A doable request might be, "The next time you're getting feedback on your project in the team meeting, would you be willing to reflect back your understanding of the feedback to check if you understood it as intended before you react?"

This is a doable request that the boss might make, imagining that this might meet his needs for effectiveness and collaboration.

Mindful Practice

In the week ahead, notice the requests you are making. Are they actually doable? If not, how might you rephrase the request so it is doable?

"Often when we think of making a request, it stems first from noticing that somebody is doing something that we don't want." (Page 53)

TIP #24: TELL ME WHAT YOU WANT!

Formulating a request in *action language* means that we say what it is we want as opposed to *what we don't want.*

It's common to think of making a request out of noticing what we don't want. For example, you and your coworker get in an argument, and your coworker is speaking louder than you would like. Your first response might be, "Would you please stop yelling?" This is an example of what you don't want—yelling.

In this case, what is it that you *do want?* Maybe your request is, "Would you be willing to speak at a volume level that matches what I'm using right now?" or "Would you be willing to be silent for the next minute?"

If you notice that your request is stated in terms of what you *do not want,* take a minute to translate it into what you *do want.*

Mindful Practice

This week, notice the language of a request you make of a colleague. Is your language focused on what you do not want instead of what you do want? How might you rephrase your request in action language?

"We all know that life can get in the way of the best-laid plans." (Page 55)

TIP #25: WHAT DO YOU WANT RIGHT NOW?

"Get the report done by Friday" or "Meet the client for lunch by the end of the month" sound like reasonable requests.

Yet any number of situations may arise to prevent you from fulfilling these requests—there may be a natural disaster, a personal or family crisis, or a less extreme situation that likewise precludes fulfilling the original intention. If taken literally, asking someone to agree or promise to get the report to you by five o'clock on Friday is to ask them to commit to something they do not have the physical capacity to guarantee will happen.

Instead, phrase your request in the present tense, asking their present intention to do something in the future. "Are you willing to agree now to get the report to me by Friday afternoon?" While subtle, this distinction offers much more clarity of what we're actually asking for *right now*. It can help us avoid unnecessary conflict because our agreements are clear.

Mindful Practice

Think of a recent request you made of someone. What, if anything, needs to change for it to be doable, in the present tense, and in action language?

"When you ask a person to tell you how they feel having heard what you've said, you are in a sense seeking to measure the quality of the connection between you." (Page 57)

TIP #26: WHAT TYPE OF REQUEST IS THAT?

Do you find yourself getting mixed up at the point of making a request? Are you unclear how to formulate the language in the moment and in a manner that ensures your request is clear?

Sometimes thinking about the general categories requests naturally fall into can help you effectively formulate the best way of expressing the request. Here are the three types of requests:

1. **Action Requests:** Ask for a change in behavior, either from another person or from yourself. These are the requests that, if met, you imagine will meet your needs. "Would you be willing to get me a glass of water?"

2. **Process Requests**: The two types of process requests ask a person to tell you either what they've just heard you say or how they feel having heard what you've just said.

   - When you ask a person to tell you how they feel having heard what you've said, you are in a sense seeking to measure the quality of the connection between you.

- When you ask a person to tell you what they heard you say, you can think of it as a means of assessing whether the message you sent was received as you intended it to be.

Mindful Practice

In the week ahead, imagine how you might insert a process request into a conversation you had recently or one that is upcoming. How might this type of request contribute to connection and clarity?

"Our task in getting clear about our needs and requests and formulating doable, present tense, action-language requests is to have as few assumptions implicit in the request as possible." (Page 62)

TIP #27: WATCH OUT FOR ASSUMPTIONS!

When making requests, we often use language that has a lot of assumptions, and thereby a lot of ambiguity. For instance, your boss may say, "Keep me in the loop," regarding a project you just reported on. What is it specifically she is requesting?

Your boss might mean for you to notify her of any changes in the plan, but you might assume she means for you to email her every day with your progress. This ambiguity can lead to conflict simply because what is being said isn't as clear as it could be.

In the workplace, have you ever wanted something and have even talked about it with coworkers, without actually stating the request? If you get the sense or hear someone is trying to make a request, and you want certainty and clarity about it, then try reflecting your understanding of the request back to them, translating what you've heard into present tense, action-oriented, doable language.

In this way, you increase the likelihood that you will get your needs met and help others get theirs met through clear communication.

Mindful Practice

This week, listen carefully for the requests behind simple or vague statements from coworkers or your boss. Try reflecting back what you hear to create more clarity between you.

"Any time we label someone in a static way, we limit their full humanity and then tend to interact with them out of this diminished idea of who they are." (Page 64)

TIP #28: WHO ARE YOUR WORKPLACE ENEMIES?

You might be thinking, "But I don't have any enemies, I get along with everyone!"

The phrase "enemy image" is borrowed from Dr. Marshall Rosenberg, founder of Nonviolent Communication. You carry an enemy image of someone anytime you have a moralistic judgment, diagnosis, or analysis of someone else or yourself as a thought in your head.

"She's incompetent," "He's a control freak," or even "I screwed up" are statements that limit the humanity of the person in question. And once we've assigned these labels, we tend to interact with the person out of this diminished idea of who they are.

Let's say you actually think your boss is a jerk. As long as you don't act on this thought, it's harmless, right? Not necessarily. Think about how this label might limit your perception of their potential or your interpretation of their actions. If you've ever had a label assigned to you in the workplace, you might remember how this label felt limiting to you as well.

Remember, your thoughts affect your feeling state, which in turn affect the rhythm of your speech, the words you choose, and the energy with which you deliver them.

Mindful Practice

This week, choose a recent judgmental thought of yourself or someone else, like "I screwed up" or "That person is impossible." While holding that thought in your mind, ask yourself, "What need am I seeking to meet by having that thought?"

"I have an enemy image whenever I have a judgment, diagnosis, or analysis of someone else or myself as a thought in my head." (Page 63)

TIP #29: HOW DO YOU SEE YOUR BOSS?

When someone has authority over you (like your boss), you often hold certain beliefs and judgments about them. These judgments can affect how you interact and often have a negative effect on your productivity and certainly your enjoyment of work. How is your image of your boss or another authority figure impacting you?

To transform this enemy image back into something that contributes to your enjoyment of work, you first need to remember that your enemy image is just an expression of your unmet need. Instead of putting the focus on the image itself or the person it's directed to, take your thoughts inward.

As you express this enemy image or judgment, what is the need of yours that is unmet? Try moving through a list of needs gently, seeing which one resonates the most with you. You'll begin to feel satisfied with this part of the process when you feel a certain resonance with your guess, often accompanied by a marked change in your felt sense.

Mindful Practice

In the week ahead, think of one instance where using the enemy image process might come in handy and utilize it. What was the outcome?

"We are more likely to get our needs met when we are sufficiently open to hearing and connecting with the needs of others." (Page 70)

TIP #30: EMPATHIZING WITH THE ENEMY

Tip #29 talked about using silent empathy to connect to the needs behind an enemy image you might harbor for an authority figure at work. To complete this process, it's important to also empathize with the "enemy" her- or himself.

Let's say you've deemed someone as a "micro-manager." You might discover that behind this judgment are your own needs for autonomy and trust. You know you work far more creatively and produce much better results when you can work on your own. And you want your boss to trust you'll follow through on your work.

Now, to work toward really transforming that enemy image entirely, it's important to connect to your boss's needs behind what you interpret as her "micromanagement" strategy. As you explore what she might need, examine how your own state of mind and physical presence might shift. You may even notice the enemy image dropping away entirely, and instead you begin to see a *human* standing in front of you.

Mindful Practice

In the week ahead, make a conscious effort to recognize even subtle enemy images you may have in place toward coworkers or authority figures at work. Explore the process of silent empathy and empathy and see how it might open up new possibilities for your relationship with the person in question.

"When we anticipate that an interaction might be complicated, there are steps we can take to engage with the other person in ways that are more likely to be satisfying." (Pages 70–71)

TIP #31: THERE ISN'T ANYTHING EASY ABOUT IT

You know those quintessential "difficult work conversations"—the interactions no one really enjoys having but are often considered just part of the job? Or conversations you feel you must have to address a conflict that's affecting productivity?

Do you wish you could face this type of conversation with a little more confidence?

Try these steps:

Step 1: Address Your Enemy Images
Ensure your openness for possibility in the conversation by making sure there are no enemy images, using Tips 29 and 30.

Step 2: Reflect on What You Learned Doing Step 1
You will probably realize that you have changed how you thought about this situation from before you started Step 1 to after completing it. Can you put into words what you have experienced—what you learned by doing Step 1?

Step 3: Practice a Conversation Role-Play
If you're worried about getting triggered during the conversation, practice it out loud with a trusted friend or colleague. Practice responding to some potential things the other party might say that are likely to trigger you.

Mindful Practice

Are you facing a difficult conversation? In the week ahead, try the steps above. As you do, ask yourself: Does my confidence or comfort in facing the conversation begin to shift?

"The underlying intention in using NVC is to connect—for each of us to connect with ourselves and with others. Out of this connection, we can create mutually satisfying outcomes." (Page 5)

TIP #32: A NEW KIND OF MEETING PREP

Are you going to communicate some hard-to-hear information to your employees or coworkers? Perhaps it's news of a layoff, a change in employee benefits, or something worse?

In your desire to consider the impact of a hard decision on the employee, you might forget to check in with the relationship between the news you have to share and your own values.

If you find yourself facing a difficult decision or potentially painful news you're planning to communicate, take a new approach to prepare for this meeting. Check in with yourself using self-empathy. Uncover your own feelings about the news and the needs that are met or not met in your sharing of it, especially in relationship to your core values as a leader.

As you work through this check-in, write out what you discover on paper. Hopefully, this process of reflection will be enough to reground you in your needs, helping you stay grounded even if the recipients of your message respond with anger, pain, or judgment.

Mindful Practice

This week, make the intention to engage in at least ten minutes of self-empathy before going into a difficult conversation. Notice any change you experience in the meeting itself.

"NVC is simple, but not easy." (Page 8)

TIP #33: WHAT DID YOU LEARN?

You made it through the tough conversation with a coworker—congratulations. And in hindsight you think it went really well. But what did you learn as a result?

A great method to continue building on your NVC practice in the workplace is to take a few minutes after each difficult conversation and conduct a quick conversation debrief, either alone or with your practice partner.

Write down your observations of your behavior prior to the meeting (did you do something different to prepare that you discovered was very effective?) and how you felt entering the meeting.

Do the same for the meeting itself. Can you think of one thing that happened that you want to celebrate? One thing you want to mourn that you wish could have gone better?

If you find you are judging yourself or others in the meeting, pause to inquire what needs you are seeking to meet by having those judgments. Each time you conduct this type of debrief, you'll further build your emotional vocabulary, and further ingrain the process and consciousness into your natural communication patterns.

Mindful Practice

This week, practice a conversation debrief for any workplace conversation that stands out in your mind, either on paper alone or aloud with your practice partner.

"Even with my intention being to fulfill needs for fun and play, however, other people may still be distressed by my humor." (Page 75)

TIP #34: THAT'S NOT FUNNY!

Humor can be tricky in the workplace. While having fun at work is a value few would argue against, some statements and jokes—or how either is expressed—can result in more complaints than laughter, contributing to the creation of an uncomfortable or even a hostile workplace.

How do you address humor in the workplace? How do you hold the need for fun and play with the need for safety, comfort, or trust at the same time?

Ask yourself: "What is your primary intention behind the type of humor you use in the workplace? Is it for fun and play? Is it expressed out of nervousness and a desire for belonging or acceptance? Or something else?

"My guess is that if I have any other intention in using humor, such as an intention to instruct, or any sense of wanting to punish, criticize, or undermine anyone with my humor, it is more likely to trigger a reaction in somebody else" (page 75).

Another important question to ask yourself is, "How is your humor received?" Do the recipients of your humor fully connect with your intention, or are they feeling something quite different?

Mindful Practice

This week, think about your own or someone else's humorous statements and connect with the intention behind them. What needs do you guess this humor is intended to meet?

"Even if you are not a facilitator of a meeting, there are ways that you can help meetings become more satisfying to you." (Page 82)

TIP #35: THIS MEETING IS A COMPLETE WASTE OF TIME!

Chances are, you've found yourself expressing your frustration about a meeting at one time or another. From meetings that seem to have no clear purpose or direction to meetings where a participant has talked long past your willingness to stay engaged, meetings have gotten a bad rap.

Even if you're not leading the meeting, though, you can still help meetings be more effective. One strategy is interrupting, a step that can be intimidating to some because it can be seen as rude and lead to further disconnect instead of the clarity and efficiency you seek.

Before you interrupt, get clear on what needs you are hoping to meet by interrupting. Is it clarity about what the person is saying, about what that person wants, or is it a need for efficiency (to share that you understand and wish to move on)?

Use silent empathy in the moment to connect to the needs behind your discomfort and desire to interrupt.

Mindful Practice

This week, during a meeting, take notice of your feelings during the meeting. Do you find yourself comfortable and engaged with the meeting direction and flow, or do you find yourself tense, uncomfortable, anxious? What needs might be behind these feelings?

"First get clear on what needs you will meet by interrupting." (Page 82)

TIP #36: "MAY I INTERRUPT YOU?"

Tip #35 suggested pausing before you interrupt in a meeting to get clear on your intention and the needs that might be met with such an action. Let's take this concept a little further.

"Knowing your needs helps you know what you will ask; the person speaking may initially be irritated when you interrupt, so you will want to have a specific connecting request ready, perhaps even tied to your needs" (page 82).

For instance, if a person has talked far longer than you've enjoyed, you might ask what she wishes the group do with the information she's shared. In other words, you ask her to *clarify her request to the group.*

Be prepared that your interruption might be met with initial irritation or even confusion, and this often stems from our desire to be heard. In other cases, the person may believe they've already made a request of the group, when the reality is that the group only heard a series of observations or ideas.

Try to reflect back what you heard the person say so far. This reframing will likely help her get to the gist of her message, giving her an opportunity to further clarify or the confidence that she has indeed been heard. Either way, both are likely to move the conversation forward in a manner that better meets everyone's needs.

Mindful Practice

This week, find an opportunity to practice reflecting what you heard a person say. Notice their response and where it takes your conversation.

"Helping others [make clear requests] is a key way you can contribute in a meeting." (Page 83)

TIP #37: LISTEN FOR THE "PLEASE" OR "THANK YOU"

In every workplace conversation, a person is always saying one of two things: please or thank you. When you're stuck in a meeting that isn't progressing in a way you enjoy, try to determine which of these the speaker is expressing.

If you think someone is saying "please," try to guess their request if it isn't clear. Modeling a clear request with a guess is a great way to help your colleague actually get what they want too.

Ask the speaker questions to help formulate a doable, present tense, action-language request. Take care that the request meets these criteria rather than stating a general assumption like "We'll get that done" or "I'd like you to take care of it."

"Helping others in a group clarify their requests helps get those requests met, which builds rapport and trust within the group" (page 83).

Mindful Practice

In the week ahead, continue to build your meeting skills; watch for opportunities to model a clear, doable, present-tense, action-language request . . . and take it!

"We tend to get highly triggered when we think that someone knows our needs are not being met but is doing nothing about it." (Page 86)

TIP #38: "I CAN'T ASK FOR THAT!"

Power differentials definitely exist in the workplace, but our perceptions of their extent or of our choices in association with them can often be more perception than reality.

Regardless, the impact of these perceptions can keep you struggling to meet your fundamental needs. Needs for safety and security of livelihood get in the way of approaching a person who is perceived to hold power. We tell ourselves, "I just can't ask for that."

Think of a current workplace situation where you've been fearful to ask for something from your boss that would help meet your needs. In one context, you think the person might not know your needs are not met and you're unsure how to tell him. In another context, you're sure he knows but he seems insensitive to the fact.

In either case, you might find yourself highly triggered and thereby reluctant to make the request. Self-empathy can play a powerful role in helping you separate perception from reality, and in turn, help you gain more comfort in asking for what you need.

Mindful Practice

In the week ahead, explore your comfort level making a request to your boss. What perceptions or beliefs are behind this level of comfort or discomfort?

"Nonviolent Communication is not a magic wand that you can wave when you are afraid that the person you are talking with will not receive you in the way that you would like." (Page 87)

TIP #39: WHEN IT DOESN'T WORK

The fact is, as you build your NVC skills and consciousness there will be plenty of instances where your "best NVC" doesn't produce the kind of results you'd hoped for. In fact, it may produce quite the opposite.

Self- and silent empathy can be powerful tools to reconnect you with your intention in just about any situation. They help pull us out of that uncomfortable and highly unproductive self-talk that often stems from frustration, such as "This NVC stuff just doesn't work" or "Why is this so hard" or even "Why don't any of them hear me?"

With self- or silent empathy, you might discover other ways to get your needs met, or you might even decide that you need to remove yourself from the situation altogether. Either way, this reconnection to your basic human needs will take you back to a state of choice.

Mindful Practice

Finding yourself frustrated by your NVC progress? This week, pause and engage in self- or silent empathy deliberately. Do you notice a shift in your sense of hope and commitment to the process?

"When people repeat gossip about another person, they are attempting to establish common norms or see if you share their same set of values." (Page 88)

TIP #40: THE COMPLAINT DEPARTMENT

Have you ever felt like your desk or cubicle has turned into the company complaint department? Do you often feel dragged into workplace gossip by a colleague who always seems to be complaining?

If you're tired of being the workplace complaint department, transforming it starts by viewing the "complaint" itself in a new light.

Complaints are tragic expressions of unmet needs—tragic because the complaint is usually laden with judgment and is often directed to whoever will listen, rather than the person eliciting the pain in the first place.

When a colleague shares a judgment-laden story about a coworker, they're likely trying to see if you share their values. Their complaint is their way of checking in.

"Did you hear she didn't get along with anyone at her last job?" might translate to "Do you share my values for trust and mutual respect?" In this manner, suddenly a gossipy complaint turns into an opportunity for connection.

Mindful Practice

This week, make an intention to translate a complaint into a check-in on shared values. Translate the complaint using silent empathy or check in with your coworker directly. How does this step affect the conversation?

"In getting the other person to agree with our judgments, we get a kind of empathy, but not a fully satisfying one, as we have not yet connected to our needs." (Page 88)

TIP #41: TRANSFORMING WORKPLACE GOSSIP

Have you ever found yourself in the middle of workplace gossip? Your coworker relays yet another anxiety-ridden story about an interaction she had with your boss. You want her to know you've heard her, but you also want to meet your needs for honesty, transparency, and respect.

Similar to how you translate a complaint, think of this piece of gossip as an opportunity for connection, too, where you can use empathy to connect without agreeing to the judgment she's communicating. At the heart of stories like this is a coworker trying to measure their sense of reality.

Here's an example: "Did you hear about Joe stealing from the supply room?" might translate to "Did you also experience a sense of distrust learning that someone has stolen supplies from the office?"

Next time you hear a story like this, instead of agreeing to the judgment, meet both of your needs by using empathy.

Mindful Practice

This week, search for opportunities to translate a piece of gossip back into needs. Check in with your coworker and take note of the impact your empathic connection has on your interaction.

> **"Feedback . . . often brings up our needs for safety and security, occurring as it does in relationship to our livelihood."** (Page 92)

TIP #42: WHAT'S YOUR PERCEPTION?

In the workplace, continual, constructive feedback is essential to helping you do your job effectively. But more often than not, feedback comes far too little (such as only in the form of an annual employee evaluation) and/or in a manner that is vague, judgment-laden, or simply not actionable.

"All too often what we call feedback is loaded with judgments about the other person or ourselves" (page 91). Think of statements like "You're not a team player," "You need to step up to the plate," or "You need to be more aware of people's feelings."

It's no wonder that most of us have been taught to perceive feedback as negative. And in the workplace, we're taught to associate employee evaluations with anxiety, especially when their outcome will affect our financial security.

Reflect on the feedback you recently gave a colleague or an employee. What did you express? If you had received this same feedback yourself, how would you have interpreted it?

Mindful Practice

This week, explore on paper all of the perceptions and associations you currently have about the terms "employee feedback" or "annual employee evaluations." What did you come up with?

"Feedback is often one of the most problematic pieces of communication." (Page 91)

TIP #43: TELL ME HOW YOU REALLY FEEL

In many cases, we're restricted in how we give feedback because of the process or format our workplace requires us to follow, such as a rating or checkbox type of system. We might find ourselves caught in a cycle of communicating judgments, with no direct tie to specific behavior.

"In workplace evaluations, feedback often takes on a higher level of importance without a corresponding increase in its clarity or usefulness" (page 92).

Regardless of the system you're required to use, you can create more meaningful feedback by using the tools of NVC, including tying feedback to a specific observation and what needs were met or not met in the process.

In this case a low rating on the teamwork scale could be augmented with an observation and link to needs, such as specific observations you've had of the quality of work relationships, communication, or productivity you've observed as they've worked in a group. In this manner, the individual has context for the rating you've given them and how their own behavior compared to your expectations, your needs, and those of the rest of the workplace team.

Mindful Practice

Think of someone you give feedback to or receive feedback from. How might you clarify the feedback using the distinctions of NVC?

"If you find yourself triggered by the feedback, practice self-empathy to reconnect with your own needs." (Page 98)

TIP #44: ASK FOR IT!

Have you found yourself feeling confused, frustrated, or even defensive when you've received feedback from a boss or coworker?

Chances are their feedback was communicated as a judgment without a link to specific observations or behavior, leaving you wondering where or how they came up with the judgment in the first place.

If you receive feedback that leaves you triggered or confused, practice self-empathy to reconnect with your needs or take a time-out if you need to do self-empathy away from the person. Then use silent empathy to guess the needs the other person is trying to meet with their evaluation.

Try restating what you've heard in observation and needs language and check if you've heard the other person correctly. You might then see if the other person has a request for different behavior from you, and you can help them arrive at that by offering some guesses. In this way you can transform a negative, vague judgment into a highly empowered conversation for both parties.

Mindful Practice

This week, think about a negative evaluation you've received recently. How might you have heard this differently if it were stated in observation and needs language?

"Taking the time to acknowledge and celebrate both individual and group accomplishments helps build group cohesion and increases individual satisfaction." (Page 83)

TIP #45: REMEMBER TO CELEBRATE!

Does the feedback you provide typically focus on the things you'd like to see change and less on the things you really enjoy?

In the workplace, it's just as important to provide observations of positive behavior that meets your needs. These celebrations can significantly enhance team dynamics and morale, while offering continued clarity about what's working well.

Positive feedback can be communicated in much the same manner as you describe negative feedback. Start with a clear observation, absent of judgment, and link that behavior to the needs of yours that were met.

For instance, instead of "You did a really great job on that proposal," you might say, "I'm really excited by the volume of background research and supporting information you included in your proposal. I know how important this level of detail is to this particular client, and your work will make our job of pitching our services in person so much easier."

Mindful Practice

In the week ahead, watch for opportunities to provide positive feedback to celebrate a job well done in observation and needs language. Notice how the message affects the recipient.

"If you enjoyed an interaction with a coworker, then you will be celebrating the needs met. Think about what specific observations you can make . . ." (Page 22)

TIP #46: THAT'S UNACCEPTABLE BEHAVIOR!

In the workplace, we have many layers of agreements between supervisors and staff, between coworkers, and between employees and their customers. These written—and more often, *unwritten*—agreements play an important role in maintaining a positive work environment.

What do you do when such an agreement has been broken? For instance, let's say you have an agreement that your employee will immediately greet all customers coming into the store with a greeting, followed by asking, "May I help you find something?"

Yet several times this week you observed customers lingering at the front counter waiting several minutes for help. Your agreement has been broken, so how do you respond? In many cases your first response might be one of judgment: "Doesn't he get it? Making customers wait for help is just unacceptable!"

As soon as you recognize your judgments and distress, ideally before communicating with the other person, do the enemy image process. Take the time to clarify what needs are not met before you communicate anything, and then include your observations and needs when you talk to the other person.

Mindful Practice

Think of a recent time that someone broke an agreement with you. Use the enemy image process, then practice what you might say to them.

"When we inquire about the needs someone is seeking to meet by their conduct, we inquire about something that we can in fact have some leverage with." (Page 100)

TIP #47: WHAT'S YOUR REALITY?

The last tip talked about using the enemy image process as the first step in responding to a broken agreement; to take a quick time-out and confirm what needs of yours are not met by the broken agreement, and in doing so, to translate any judgment you may be having about it.

Now that you're thinking more clearly about the broken agreement, it's important to check if you and the other person have a shared understanding of what the agreement was in the first place.

"John, my understanding was that you agreed to greet anyone who walks into the store right away by saying 'Hello' and asking if you could help them find anything. Yet, on several occasions this week I've noticed customers at the front counter not being served for several minutes. Can you tell me what's been going on for you that has kept you from greeting customers more quickly?"

By stating your observation in this way, you're trying to bring out any assumptions and thereby confirm if you have a shared reality. And by asking him to help you understand *his* experience, you invite him to share the needs he's meeting with his current behavior (albeit in colloquial language). In this way your starting point is one of inquiry rather than finality, which is far more likely to ultimately lead to the behavior you'd like.

Mindful Practice

Continue your thought about a recent time that someone broke an agreement with you. How might a check-in to see if you had the same understanding of your agreements change the conversation?

"At the heart of the intention to connect is being connected—in a visceral, noncognitive way—with yourself, which is to say with your own needs." (Page 6)

TIP #48: CLEAN UP YOUR MESS!

Another common workplace issue that provides opportunities to practice your new skills and get your needs met is the orderliness of shared areas.

"It seems that in every workplace, there are the neatniks and those who are not so neat. When the neatniks have had enough of dirty coffee mugs left in the sink, screaming signs are posted demanding that the not-neatniks clean up their dishes" (page 97).

Likely a different approach, leveraging the intentions behind NVC, will result in a more positive response. Instead of a screaming sign demanding a quick clean-up, try to communicate to your coworkers in observation language, followed by the need of yours that is not met and ending with a request.

For instance: "When I see you prepare your lunch in the kitchen and leave your dishes in the sink unwashed, I feel frustrated because my need for respect is not met. Would you be willing to commit to rinsing your dishes and putting them in the dishwasher after your meal?"

Mindful Practice

Choose a recurring issue in your workplace. How might you approach it differently using your new skills?

"Many of us receive more email daily than we enjoy, and here again is an opportunity to develop fluency and ease with Nonviolent Communication." (Page 102)

TIP #49: DON'T HIT THE "SEND" BUTTON YET . . .

In our fast-paced, electronic world, the one-way nature of email communication can often lead to unintentional conflict. In our desire for efficiency and productivity, many emails offer more confusion than clarity.

Think about an email you've received recently that left you triggered. Perhaps you perceived quite a bit of pain in the email, or it's brevity left you confused.

Before you pound out a response and hit the "send" button, take a pause. Just like a live interaction that might leave you triggered, an immediate response to an email that has left you triggered is likely to be unproductive.

Use self-empathy to check in to your feelings and needs. Next, use empathy to guess the needs of the person who wrote the email. What do you discover in this process?

Mindful Practice

This week, challenge yourself to pause before you reply to any email that leaves you triggered or confused. How does this pause affect the quality of your response?

"I notice that when I am living out of judgments, I tend to create outcomes that are missing something." (Page 168)

TIP #50: LET'S TRY A DIFFERENT WAY . . .

Have you experienced some frustration initiating change in your workplace, particularly in introducing new or different ways to communicate?

Introducing a new way of doing things in the workplace can be tough. We often fall into self-limiting patterns (of behavior, perception, and relationships) because we have beliefs about what we can or cannot do in the workplace. We get wrapped up in expectations around these beliefs, especially in what others might think of us if we did things in a different way.

"In our workplaces, we often create an illusion of separateness and formality that then reinforces our beliefs in this regard and thereby results in our acting in more confining ways" (page 165).

Do you have self-limiting beliefs or assumptions about your workplace culture and/or the expectations of those you work with? Challenge yourself to explore these beliefs on paper. Are they hindering your ability to model a different way of doing things?

Mindful Practice

This week be aware of your self-limiting beliefs regarding "how things are done" in your workplace. As these beliefs come up, notice how they might affect your willingness to model to your colleagues a more fulfilling way of communicating.

"The premise of NVC is that when you focus on connection with yourself and others, you will be meeting your needs while, at the same time, others in your world are meeting their needs." (Page 8)

TIP #51: REMEMBER THE FOUR CHOICES

There are many opportunities to practice NVC in the workplace, many of which don't require you to speak at all: a team meeting, an email you receive from a customer, your morning commute, even a direct interaction with your boss.

It's helpful to remember that in any interaction you have four choices in how to respond:

1. **Self-empathy:** Inquire into what is going on with yourself
2. **Silent empathy**: Guess silently what is going on with the other person
3. **Empathy**: Guess out loud what is going on with the other person
4. **Expression**: Share out loud with the other person what is going on for you, including your observation, feelings, needs, and request.

If you find yourself stuck in a situation or interaction at work, go back to this list of four choices. Which would provide you some valuable insight?

Mindful Practice

In the week ahead, take notice of moments where you're unsure how best to respond to a challenging situation or interaction. Explore using each of the four choices. What effect do you observe for each on the quality of the connection?

"NVC is not only about how I use language to communicate with myself (i.e., how I think) and with others (i.e., how I speak), but about how I filter my perception of the sensory inputs from the world inside and outside of me." (Page viii)

TIP #52: REMEMBER YOUR INTENTION

As you work to continue to practice and strengthen your application of NVC in the workplace, you're bound to come across some challenging moments.

As these arise, it's important to remember that NVC is simply a tool to reconnect you to your own needs and those of others. The structure is a way to remind you to stay focused on the present moment.

If you go into a future situation with a mental model of the structure—(I'll do self-empathy and feel compassion; then I'll be curious about the other person and do silent empathy and feel more compassion; then I'll be able to have a conversation in which I'll stay curious about the other person"—you've taken your attention away from the present moment.

Instead, always focus on what is going on for you in the present moment, and use the structure to *work with your* experience, not try to fit your experience into the structure.

Ultimately, "NVC is not about changing the way you talk; it's about changing the way you think and the way you view the world" (page 168).

Mindful Practice

In the week ahead, check in with your intention as you take part in various workplace interactions. What does your intention tell you about what is occupying your attention?

Conclusion

We tend to have a certain type of relationship with our coworkers. We spend a lot of time with them (sometimes even more than with our family), yet keep a certain distance; these are not usually our most intimate relationships. The distance we maintain from coworkers, combined with the particular culture in our organization, can make introducing a new way of doing things seem daunting.

What I've learned (from my own experience, from conducting workshops, and from coaching and mediating workplace issues) is that we often fall into self-limiting patterns based on our beliefs about what we can and cannot do in the workplace. We think others have expectations about acceptable ways to talk or act, and then we follow those without necessarily checking to see how accurate our understanding of these expectations is. In our workplaces, we often create an illusion of separateness and formality that then reinforces our beliefs in this regard and thereby results in our acting in more confining ways. In workshops I have seen over and over again that when people do their own self- and silent empathy work at a deep level, they realize that they are not limited by what they can say in the workplace. I think what they begin to see—even those who come to a workshop absolutely hopeless about being able to apply Nonviolent Communication in a work setting—is that people are people, whether they are at work or elsewhere.

If you have arrived at the point of wanting to integrate NVC into your life, then the workplace is one of the places to do it. Julie Greene, an NVC trainer, once told me that at one point she just decided to "jump off the cliff" and use NVC in all of her interactions with people. She assumed she would make some messes, and would then use those messes as opportunities for further practice. By "messes," I think she meant that people would sometimes react to the new way she was interacting, and she would then need to find a way to reconnect with them. I liked this image of jumping off the cliff—at that point, I myself stopped making any differentiation between how I communicated at work and in my personal life.

I hope that in this book you have seen that there are many opportunities to use NVC in the workplace without necessarily doing something out loud that coworkers will identify as a process. These silent skills can provide stepping-stones to transition to using more out loud skills. Whether you decide to use NVC out loud or only silently, NVC can always be used as a self-care process to support your own learning, especially in managing the sometimes difficult situations that arise in the course of your day.

If we are within the NVC model, we have four choices at any one moment to respond to what is happening within or without. Two of these choices are silent, two are out loud. The silent choices are self-empathy and silent empathy, which we discussed in Chapter 2. The out loud choices are empathy and expression: In empathy, we guess what might be going on for the other person. In expression, we share with the other person what is going on for us—our own Observations, Feelings, Needs, and Requests.

If you look back through this book, you'll see that you can deconstruct everything back to these four basic choices. Some of the topics we cover, such as the enemy image process, are simply names put to a particular way of structuring these basic choices or a particular purpose for using them. If you have a quandary about what to do in a situation in the workplace, you can use these choices to decide on a way to proceed. I would suggest that you start with self-empathy or find another way to get your need for empathy met first; reconnecting with yourself is fundamental, and without that, any other choice you make is more likely to come from reaction rather than connection to your needs. When you are connected with your own needs, the natural next choice is often silent empathy. Following that, you might inquire internally whether you then want to use one of the out loud choices of empathy or expression as a strategy to meet your needs. I have used this way of thinking about my choices, in any situation, for years; when I perceive I'm stuck or at a loss for what to do, using this simple model has helped me find my way out every time. Practicing each of these four choices will help you remember in each moment that you have this toolkit to choose from. As you gain skill in each one, you will learn that there are all kinds of permutations to how you can use them, and you will begin to learn when and in what order to use them depending on the situation.

You have probably noticed that I've given a basic structure to the experience of using these four choices, then applied that structure over and over again to many different workplace situations. What I hope you come away with, however, is that this structure is really like pointing a finger at the moon; you want to look at the moon, not the finger. The structure is simply a way to remind you to stay focused on the present moment. If you go into a situation with a mental model of the structure—"I'll do self-empathy and feel compassion; then I'll be curious about the other person and do silent empathy and feel more compassion; then I'll be able to have a conversation in which I'll stay curious about the other person"—and expect your experience to follow it, then you'll be trying to live in the image, not in the present. The process of giving ourselves or another person empathy, going through the learning cycle, or working with enemy images is always just that—a process. Especially when you are first practicing these skills, there may be many iterations of guessing feelings and needs before identifying those that hit home, and those iterations may happen over minutes, days, or even weeks. It may take more than one session of empathy for yourself before you can even imagine feeling curious about the other person. Even after you have empathized with yourself and the other person, compassion may or may not arise. No part of this structure of experience is a given; what we most want is for you to be aware of what is going on for you in the present moment, each present moment—and to use the structure to work with your experience, not try to fit your experience into the structure.

Finally, I'd like to leave you with the reminder that NVC is not about changing the way you talk; it's about changing the way you think and the way you view the world. That is no small undertaking. You may well want a support team—one or more individuals that you trust to help you in this process. These people can also remind you that these kinds of fundamental changes do not happen overnight; most often it's a long process of practice, making mistakes, and getting disconnected and reconnected over and over and over again.

Nonetheless, it's worth it. I trust in the kind of world that my conduct will be contributing to when I translate my judgments into observations, identify my needs met or not met, and make requests in the world based on those. The results are far more satisfying. I realize now how disconnected I am from myself and others when I live out of judgments rather than needs, and I notice that when I am living out of judgments, I tend to create outcomes that are missing something. Those outcomes tend to have buried consequences that don't meet my needs. Besides, I have grown to enjoy learning how inaccurate my judgments often are.

The reason that I make the effort to write this, to incorporate NVC into my life, and to make NVC my work is because I want to be part of creating a world that is characterized by the arising of compassion. Nonviolent Communication is not the only path to this goal, but it is the one that I have found the most useful for me. I share this work with you in the hopes that it resonates; that we all can work toward creating this world for our children, for all children, and for all of us.

Appendix A: Training Wheels Sentence

EXPRESSING COMPASSIONATELY

1. Identify the observable behavior.

When I
{
see
hear
remember
imagine
}
_____

2. Express my feelings.

I feel _____

3. Communicate my need/preference.

Because I would have liked

Because
I was
{
needing
hoping
wanting
}
_____

4. Make a request in present tense, action language.

And right now, would you be willing to tell me
(a) what you heard me say?
(b) how you feel hearing what I just said?
(c) if you are willing to say or do the following?_____

RECEIVING EMPATHICALLY

1. Guess the observable behavior.

When you { see / hear / remember / imagine } _____

Or

Are you reacting to / Are you talking about / Are you referring to } _____

2. Guess the other person's feelings.

Are you feeling / I'm guessing you're feeling } _____

3. Guess the other person's unmet need/preference.

Because you would have liked / Because you are needing } _____

4. Guess what the other person's request might be.

So now, are you wanting / And now, would you like me to } _____

Appendix B: Feelings List

absorbed	ardent	compassionate
ache	aroused	concerned
adventurous	ashamed	confident
affectionate	astonished	confused
afraid	aversion	congested
aggravated	awed	constricted
agitated	baffled	contempt
agony	beat	content
airy	bereaved	cool
alarmed	bewildered	cranky
alert	blissful	curious
alienated	bloated	damp
alive	blocked	dazed
aloof	bored	dazzled
amazed	breathless	dejected
ambivalent	brokenhearted	delighted
amused	bubbly	dense
angry	burnt out	depleted
anguished	buzzy	depressed
animated	calm	despair
animosity	centered	desperate
annoyed	chagrined	despondent
anxious	chills	detached
apathetic	clammy	devastated
appalled	clearheaded	disappointed
appreciative	cold	discombobulated
apprehensive	comfortable	disconcerted

disconnected

discouraged

disgruntled

disgusted

disheartened

dislike

dismayed

displeased

dissatisfied

distant

distracted

distraught

distressed

disturbed

dizzy

dread

dull

eager

ecstatic

edgy

elated

electric

embarrassed

empowered

enchanted

encouraged

energetic

energized

engaged

engrossed

enlivened

enraged

enthralled

enthusiastic

entranced

envious

equanimous

exasperated

excited

exhausted

exhilarated

expansive

expectant

exuberant

faint

fascinated

fatigue

fidgety

flaccid

floored

flowing

fluid

flushed

flustered

fluttery

foreboding

forlorn

fragile

frantic

frazzled

friendly

frightened

frozen

frustrated

fulfilled

furious

fuzzy

giddy

glad

gloomy

goose bumpy

grateful

grief

guarded

guilty

happy

hate

heartbroken

heavy

helpless

hesitant

hopeful

hopeless

horrified

hostile

hurt

impatient

incensed

indifferent

indignant

insecure

inspired

intense

interested	mistrustful	proud
intrigued	mixed	puffy
invigorated	moist	pulsing
involved	mortified	puzzled
irate	moved	quaky
irked	moving	quiet
irritable	mystified	quivery
irritated	nauseated	radiant
itchy	nervous	radiating
jagged	nostalgic	rapturous
jealous	numb	rattled
jittery	OK	refreshed
joyful	open	regretful
jubilant	openhearted	rejuvenated
jumbled	optimistic	relaxed
jumpy	outraged	relieved
leery	overwhelmed	remorseful
lethargic	pain	removed
light	panicked	renewed
listless	paralyzed	repulsed
lively	passionate	resentful
livid	peaceful	reserved
lonely	perplexed	rested
longing	perturbed	restless
lost	petrified	restored
loving	pining	revived
melancholy	playful	sad
mellow	pleased	safe
mild	pounding	satisfied
mischievous	pressure	scared
miserable	prickly	scattered

secure

self-conscious

sensitive

serene

shaky

sharp

shivery

shocked

shuddery

shy

sleepy

smooth

sorrowful

spacious

spasming

spellbound

spinning

startled

still

stimulated

stress

stringy

strong

suffocated

surprised

suspicious

sweaty

sympathetic

tender

tense

terrified

thankful

thick

thrilled

throbbing

tickled

tight

tightness of skin

tingly

tired

torn

touched

tranquil

tremble

tremulous

troubled

trusting

turbulent

turmoil

twitchy

uncomfortable

uneasy

unhappy

uninterested

unnerved

unsettled

upset

vibrant

vibration

vulnerable

warm

wary

weary

wistful

withdrawn

wobbly

wonder

worn out

worried

wowed

wretched

yearning

Appendix C: Feelings Versus Evaluations Masquerading as Feelings

Evaluative Word	Feeling(s)	Need(s)
abandoned	terrified, hurt, bewildered, sad, frightened, lonely	nurturing, connection, belonging, support, caring
abused	angry, frustrated, frightened	caring, nurturing, support, emotional or physical well-being, consideration, for all living things to flourish
(not) accepted	upset, scared, lonely	inclusion, connection, community, belonging, contribution, peer respect
attacked	scared, angry	safety
belittled	angry, frustrated, tense, distressed	respect, autonomy, to be seen, acknowledgment, appreciation
betrayed	angry, hurt, disappointed, enraged	trust, dependability, honesty, honor, commitment, clarity
blamed	angry, scared, confused, antagonistic, hostile, bewildered, hurt	accountability, causality, fairness, justice
bullied	angry, scared, pressured	autonomy, choice, safety, consideration
caged/boxed in	angry, thwarted, scared, anxious	autonomy, choice, freedom
cheated	resentful, hurt, angry	honesty, fairness, justice, trust, reliability
coerced	angry, frustrated, frightened, thwarted, scared	choice, autonomy, freedom (to act freely, to choose freely)

Evaluative Word	Feeling(s)	Need(s)
cornered	angry, scared, anxious, thwarted	autonomy, freedom
criticized	in pain, scared, anxious, frustrated, humiliated, angry, embarrassed	understanding, acknowledgment, recognition, accountability, nonjudgmental communication
discounted/ diminished	hurt, angry, embarrassed, frustrated	acknowledgment, inclusion, recognition, respect, to matter
disliked	sad, lonely, hurt	connection, appreciation, understanding, acknowledgment, friendship, inclusion
distrusted	sad, frustrated	trust, honesty
dumped on	angry, overwhelmed	respect, consideration
harassed	angry, frustrated, pressured, frightened	respect, space, consideration, peace
hassled	irritated, distressed, angry, frustrated	serenity, autonomy, to do things at my own pace and in my own way, calm, space
ignored	lonely, scared, hurt, sad, embarrassed	connection, belonging, inclusion, community, participation
insulted	angry, embarrassed	respect, consideration, acknowledgment, recognition
interrupted	angry, frustrated, resentful, hurt	respect, to be heard, consideration
intimidated	scared, anxious	safety, equality, empowerment

Evaluative Word	Feeling(s)	Need(s)
invalidated	angry, hurt, resentful	appreciation, respect, acknowledgment, recognition
invisible	sad, angry, lonely, scared	to be seen and heard, inclusion, belonging, community
isolated	lonely, afraid, scared	community, inclusion, belonging, contribution
left out	sad, lonely, anxious	inclusion, belonging, community, connection
let down	sad, disappointed, frightened	consistency, trust, dependability, consistency
manipulated	angry, scared, powerless, thwarted, frustrated	autonomy, empowerment, trust, equality, freedom, free choice, connection, genuineness
mistrusted	sad, angry	trust
misunderstood	upset, angry, frustrated	to be heard, understanding, clarity
neglected	lonely, scared	connection, inclusion, participation, community, care, to matter, consideration
overpowered	angry, impotent, helpless, confused	equality, justice, autonomy, freedom
overworked	angry, tired, frustrated	respect, consideration, rest, caring
patronized	angry, frustrated, resentful	recognition, equality, respect, mutuality
pressured	anxious, resentful, overwhelmed	relaxation, clarity, space, consideration

Evaluative Word	Feeling(s)	Need(s)
provoked	angry, frustrated, hostile, antagonistic, resentful	respect, consideration
put down	angry, sad, embarrassed	respect, acknowledgment, understanding
rejected	hurt, scared, angry, defiant	belonging, inclusion, closeness, to be seen, acknowledgment, connection
ripped off/ screwed	anger, resentment, disappointed	consideration, justice, fairness, acknowledgment, trust
smothered/ suffocated	frustrated, fear, desperation	space, freedom, autonomy, authenticity, self-expression
taken for granted	sad, angry, hurt, disappointed	appreciation, acknowledgment, recognition, consideration
threatened	scared, frightened, alarmed, agitated, defiant	safety, autonomy
trampled	angry, frustrated, overwhelmed	empowerment, connection, community, to be seen, consideration, equality, respect, acknowledgment
tricked	embarrassed, angry, resentful	integrity, trust, honesty
unappreciated	sad, angry, hurt, frustrated	appreciation, respect, acknowledgment, consideration
unheard	sad, hostile, frustrated	understanding, consideration, empathy

Evaluative Word	Feeling(s)	Need(s)
unloved	sad, bewildered, frustrated	love, appreciation, empathy, connection, community
unseen	sad, anxious, frustrated	acknowledgment, appreciation, to be seen and heard
unsupported	sad, hurt, resentful	support, understanding
unwanted	sad, anxious, frustrated	belonging, inclusion, caring
used	sad, angry, resentful	autonomy, equality, consideration, mutuality
victimized	frightened, helpless	empowerment, mutuality, safety, justice
violated	sad, agitated, anxious	privacy, safety, trust, space, respect
wronged	angry, hurt, resentful, irritated	respect, justice, trust, safety, fairness

*This list was developed in the April 2000 Wisconsin International Intensive, edited by Susan Skye.

Appendix D: Needs List

Connection
acceptance
affection
appreciation
be understood
belonging
closeness
communication
community
companionship
compassion
consideration
consistency
cooperation
empathy
inclusion
intimacy
love
mutuality
nurturing
respect/self-respect
safety
security
stability
support
to know and be
    known
to see and be seen
to understand and
    be understood
trust
warmth

Physical Well-Being
air
food
movement/exercise
rest/sleep
safety
sexual expression
shelter
touch
water

Honesty
authenticity
integrity
presence

Play
humor
joy

Peace
beauty
communion
ease
equality
harmony
inspiration
order

Meaning
awareness
celebration of life
challenge
clarity
competence
consciousness
contribution
creativity
discovery
effectiveness
efficacy
growth
hope
learning
mourning
participation
purpose
self-expression
stimulation
to matter
understanding

Autonomy
choice
freedom
independence
space
spontaneity

Index

The Four-Part Nonviolent Communication Process

Clearly expressing how **I am** without blaming or criticizing	Empathically receiving how **you are** without hearing blame or criticism

OBSERVATIONS

1. What I observe *(see, hear, remember, imagine, free from my evaluations)* that does or does not contribute to my well-being:

   "When I (see, hear) . . . "

1. What you observe *(see, hear, remember, imagine, free from your evaluations)* that does or does not contribute to your well-being:

   "When you see/hear . . . "

   (Sometimes unspoken when offering empathy)

FEELINGS

2. How I feel *(emotion or sensation rather than thought)* in relation to what I observe:

   "I feel . . . "

2. How you feel *(emotion or sensation rather than thought)* in relation to what you observe:

   "You feel . . ."

NEEDS

3. What I need or value *(rather than a preference, or a specific action)* that causes my feelings:

   " . . . because I need/value . . . "

3. What you need or value *(rather than a preference, or a specific action)* that causes your feelings:

   " . . . because you need/value . . ."

Clearly requesting that which would enrich **my** life without demanding	Empathically receiving that which would enrich **your** life without hearing any demand

REQUESTS

4. The concrete actions I would like taken:

   "Would you be willing to . . . ?"

4. The concrete actions you would like taken:

   "Would you like . . . ?"

   (Sometimes unspoken when offering empathy)

© Marshall B. Rosenberg. For more information about Marshall B. Rosenberg or the Center for Nonviolent Communication, please visit www.CNVC.org.

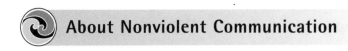

About Nonviolent Communication

Nonviolent Communication has flourished for more than four decades across sixty countries selling more than 1,000,000 books in over thirty languages for one simple reason: it works.

From the bedroom to the boardroom, from the classroom to the war zone, Nonviolent Communication (NVC) is changing lives every day. NVC provides an easy-to-grasp, effective method to get to the root of violence and pain peacefully. By examining the unmet needs behind what we do and say, NVC helps reduce hostility, heal pain, and strengthen professional and personal relationships. NVC is now being taught in corporations, classrooms, prisons, and mediation centers worldwide. And it is affecting cultural shifts as institutions, corporations, and governments integrate NVC consciousness into their organizational structures and their approach to leadership.

Most of us are hungry for skills that can improve the quality of our relationships, to deepen our sense of personal empowerment or simply help us communicate more effectively. Unfortunately, most of us have been educated from birth to compete, judge, demand, and diagnose; to think and communicate in terms of what is "right" and "wrong" with people. At best, the habitual ways we think and speak hinder communication and create misunderstanding or frustration. And still worse, they can cause anger and pain, and may lead to violence. Without wanting to, even people with the best of intentions generate needless conflict.

NVC helps us reach beneath the surface and discover what is alive and vital within us, and how all of our actions are based on human needs that we are seeking to meet. We learn to develop a vocabulary of feelings and needs that helps us more clearly express what is going on in us at any given moment. When we understand and acknowledge our needs, we develop a shared foundation for much more satisfying relationships. Join the thousands of people worldwide who have improved their relationships and their lives with this simple yet revolutionary process.

About PuddleDancer Press

PuddleDancer Press (PDP) is the main publisher of Nonviolent Communication™ related works. Its mission is to provide high-quality materials to help people create a world in which all needs are met compassionately. By working in partnership with the Center for Nonviolent Communication and NVC trainers, teams, and local supporters, PDP has created a comprehensive promotion effort that has helped bring NVC to thousands of new people each year.

Since 1998 PDP has donated more than 60,000 NVC books to organizations, decision-makers, and individuals in need around the world.

Visit the PDP website at www.NonviolentCommunication.com to find the following resources:

- **Shop NVC**—Continue your learning. Purchase our NVC titles online safely, affordably, and conveniently. Find everyday discounts on individual titles, multiple-copies, and book packages. Learn more about our authors and read endorsements of NVC from world-renowned communication experts and peacemakers. www.NonviolentCommunication.com/store/

- **NVC Quick Connect e-Newsletter**—Sign up today to receive our monthly e-Newsletter, filled with expert articles, upcoming training opportunities with our authors, and exclusive specials on NVC learning materials. Archived e-Newsletters are also available

- **About NVC**—Learn more about these life-changing communication and conflict resolution skills including an overview of the NVC process, key facts about NVC, and more.

- **About Marshall Rosenberg**—Access press materials, biography, and more about this world-renowned peacemaker, educator, bestselling author, and founder of the Center for Nonviolent Communication.

- **Free Resources for Learning NVC**—Find free weekly tips series, NVC article archive, and other great resources to make learning these vital communication skills just a little easier.

For more information, please contact PuddleDancer Press at:

2240 Encinitas Blvd., Ste. D-911 • Encinitas, CA 92024
Phone: 760-652-5754 • Fax: 760-274-6400
Email: email@puddledancer.com • www.NonviolentCommunication.com

The Center for Nonviolent Communication (CNVC) is an international nonprofit peacemaking organization whose vision is a world where everyone's needs are met peacefully. CNVC is devoted to supporting the spread of Nonviolent Communication (NVC) around the world.

Founded in 1984 by Dr. Marshall B. Rosenberg, CNVC has been contributing to a vast social transformation in thinking, speaking and acting— showing people how to connect in ways that inspire compassionate results. NVC is now being taught around the globe in communities, schools, prisons, mediation centers, churches, businesses, professional conferences, and more. Hundreds of certified trainers and hundreds more supporters teach NVC to tens of thousands of people each year in more than 60 countries.

CNVC believes that NVC training is a crucial step to continue building a compassionate, peaceful society. Your tax-deductible donation will help CNVC continue to provide training in some of the most impoverished, violent corners of the world. It will also support the development and continuation of organized projects aimed at bringing NVC training to high-need geographic regions and populations.

To make a tax-deductible donation or to learn more about the valuable resources described below, visit the CNVC website at www.CNVC.org:

- **Training and Certification**—Find local, national, and international training opportunities, access trainer certification information, connect to local NVC communities, trainers, and more.

- **CNVC Bookstore**—Find mail or phone order information for a complete selection of NVC books, booklets, audio, and video materials at the CNVC website.

- **CNVC Projects**—Participate in one of the several regional and theme-based projects that provide focus and leadership for teaching NVC in a particular application or geographic region.

- **E-Groups and List Servs**—Join one of several moderated, topic-based NVC e-groups and list servs developed to support individual learning and the continued growth of NVC worldwide.

For more information, please contact CNVC at:

9301 Indian School Rd., NE, Suite 204, Albuquerque, NM 87112-2861
Ph: 505-244-4041 • US Only: 800-255-7696 • Fax: 505-247-0414
Email: cnvc@CNVC.org • Website: www.CNVC.org

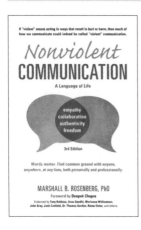

Nonviolent Communication:
A Language of Life, 3rd Edition

Life-Changing Tools for Healthy Relationships

By Marshall B. Rosenberg, PhD

$19.95 — Trade Paper 6x9, 264pp
ISBN: 978-1-892005-28-1

What is Violent Communication?

If "violent" means acting in ways that result in hurt or harm, then much of how we communicate— judging others, bullying, having racial bias, blaming, finger pointing, discriminating, speaking without listening, criticizing others or ourselves, name-calling, reacting when angry, using political rhetoric, being defensive or judging who's "good/bad" or what's "right/wrong" with people—**could indeed be called "violent communication."**

What is Nonviolent Communication?
Nonviolent Communication is the integration of four things:

- **Consciousness:** a set of principles that support living a life of compassion, collaboration, courage, and authenticity

- **Language:** understanding how words contribute to connection or distance

- **Communication:** knowing how to ask for what we want, how to hear others even in disagreement, and how to move toward solutions that work for all

- **Means of influence:** sharing "power with others" rather than using "power over others"

Nonviolent Communication serves our desire to do three things:

- **Increase our ability to live with choice, meaning, and connection**

- **Connect empathically with self and others to have more satisfying relationships**

- **Sharing of resources so everyone is able to benefit**

MORE THAN 1,000 AMAZON REVIEWS—OVER 94% 4-STAR AND 5-STAR!

Available from PuddleDancer Press, the Center for Nonviolent Communication, all major bookstores, and Amazon.com. Distributed by Independent Publisher's Group: 800-888-4741.

SAVE an extra 10% at NonviolentCommunication.com with code: **bookads**

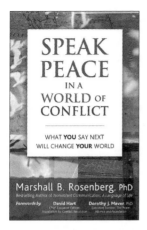

Speak Peace in a World of Conflict

What You Say Next Will Change Your World

By Marshall B. Rosenberg, PhD

$15.95 — Trade Paper 5-3/8x8-3/8, 208pp
ISBN: 978-1-892005-17-5

Create Peace in the Language You Use!

In every interaction, every conversation, and in every thought, you have a choice—to promote peace or perpetuate violence. International peacemaker, mediator, and healer, Dr. Marshall Rosenberg shows you how the language you use is the key to enriching life. Take the first step to reduce violence, heal pain, resolve conflicts, and spread peace on our planet—by developing an internal consciousness of peace rooted in the language you use each day.

Speak Peace is filled with inspiring stories, lessons, and ideas drawn from more than forty years of mediating conflicts and healing relationships in some of the most war-torn, impoverished, and violent corners of the world. *Speak Peace* offers insight, practical skills, and powerful tools that will profoundly change your relationships and the course of your life for the better.

Discover how you can create an internal consciousness of peace as the first step toward effective personal, professional, and social change. Find complete chapters on the mechanics of Speaking Peace, conflict resolution, transforming business culture, transforming enemy images, addressing terrorism, transforming authoritarian structures, expressing and receiving gratitude, and social change.

"*Speak Peace* is a book that comes at an appropriate time when anger and violence dominates human attitudes. Marshall Rosenberg gives us the means to create peace through our speech and communication. A brilliant book."

—**Arun Gandhi**, president, M. K. Gandhi Institute for Nonviolence, USA

"*Speak Peace* sums up decades of healing and peacework. It would be hard to list all the kinds of people who can benefit from reading this book, because it's really any and all of us."

—**Dr. Michael Nagler**, author, America Without Violence and Is There No Other Way: A Search for a Nonviolent Future

Available from PuddleDancer Press, the Center for Nonviolent Communication, all major bookstores, and Amazon.com. Distributed by Independent Publisher's Group: 800-888-4741.

SAVE an extra 10% at NonviolentCommunication.com with code: **bookads**

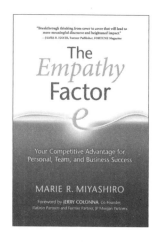

The Empathy Factor

Your Competitive Advantage for Personal, Team, and Business Success

By Marie R. Miyashiro, APR

$19.95 — Trade Paper 6x9, 256pp
ISBN: 978-1-892005-25-0

The Transformative Power of Empathy!

With In this groundbreaking book, award-winning communication and organizational strategist Marie Miyashiro explores the missing element leaders must employ to build profits and productivity in the new economy—Empathy.

Building from the latest research about organizational effectiveness, emotional aptitude in the workplace, and brain science, Miyashiro offers both real-world insight and a practical framework to bring the transformative power of empathy to your entire organization.

Miyashiro's approach combines more than 26 years of experience advising for-profit companies, government agencies, and nonprofits to substantially improve their organizational communication with a proven, world-renowned process from the largest empathy-based community in the world.

The Empathy Factor takes Dr. Marshall Rosenberg's work developing Compassionate Communication into the business community by introducing *Integrated Clarity®*—a powerful framework you can use to understand and effectively meet the critical needs of your organization without compromising those of your employees or customers.

"**Breakthrough thinking from cover to cover.** *The Empathy Factor* **will help thoughtful business people add substance and dimension to relationships within the workforce—colleagues and customers.**"

—JAMES B. HAYES, Former Publisher, FORTUNE Magazine

Available from PuddleDancer Press, the Center for Nonviolent Communication, all major bookstores, and Amazon.com. Distributed by Independent Publisher's Group: 800-888-4741.

SAVE an extra 10% at NonviolentCommunication.com with code: **bookads**

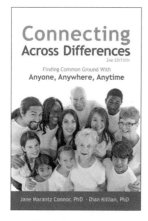

Connecting Across Differences, 2nd Edition

Finding Common Ground With Anyone, Anywhere, Anytime

By Jane Marantz Connor, PhD and Dian Killian, PhD

$19.95 — Trade Paper 6x9, 416pp
ISBN: 978-1-892005-24-3

Profound Connection Is Just a Conversation Away!

In this fully revised second edition, Dr. Dian Killian and Dr. Jane Marantz Connor offer a comprehensive and accessible guide for exploring the concepts, applications, and transformative power of the Nonviolent Communication process. Discover simple, yet transformative skills to create a life of abundance, where building the personal, professional, and community connections you long for begins with a simple shift in thinking.

Now with an expanded selection of broadly applicable exercises, role-plays, and activities that challenge readers to immediately apply the concepts in everyday life, this new edition opens the authors' insight to an even broader audience. Detailed and comprehensive, this combined book and workbook enhances communication skills by introducing the basic NVC model, as well as more advanced NVC practices.

Relevant, meaningful exercises follow each concept, giving readers the chance to immediately apply the skills they've learned to real life experiences.

Drawing on a combined 25 years of experience, the authors help readers to:

- Transform negative self-talk into self empowerment
- Foster trust and collaboration when stakes are high
- Establish healthy relationships to satisfy your needs
- Defuse anger, enemy images, and other barriers to connection
- Get what you want while maintaining respect and integrity

In each chapter, numerous exercises invite readers to apply NVC skills and concepts in their own lives. The second part features extensive dialogues illustrating NVC in action including in self-empathy, empathy, and mediation. The book closes with a resource guide for further learning and an interview with Marshall Rosenberg from the February 2003 *Sun Magazine*.

Available from PuddleDancer Press, the Center for Nonviolent Communication, all major bookstores, and Amazon.com. Distributed by Independent Publisher's Group: 800-888-4741.

SAVE an extra 10% at NonviolentCommunication.com with code: **bookads**

Being Genuine

Stop Being Nice, Start Being Real

by Thomas d'Ansembourg

$17.95 — Trade Paper 5-3/8x8-3/8, 280pp
ISBN: 978-1-892005-21-2

Being Genuine brings Thomas d'Ansembourg's blockbuster French title to the English market. His work offers you a fresh new perspective on the proven skills offered in the bestselling book, *Nonviolent Communication: A Language of Life*. Drawing on his own real-life examples and stories, Thomas d'Ansembourg provides practical skills and concrete steps that allow us to safely remove the masks we wear, which prevent the intimacy and satisfaction we desire with our intimate partners, children, parents, friends, family, and colleagues.

"Through this book, we can feel Nonviolent Communication not as a formula but as a rich, meaningful way of life, both intellectually and emotionally."

—Vicki Robin, co-founder, Conversation Cafes,
coauthor, *Your Money or Your Life*

Based on Marshall Rosenberg's Nonviolent Communication process

SAVE an extra 10% at NonviolentCommunication.com with code: **bookads**

Peaceful Living

Daily Meditations for Living With Love, Healing, and Compassion

by Mary Mackenzie

$19.95 — Trade Paper 5x7.5, 448pp
ISBN: 978-1-892005-19-9

In this gathering of wisdom, Mary Mackenzie empowers you with an intimate life map that will literally change the course of your life for the better. Each of the 366 meditations includes an inspirational quote and concrete, practical tips for integrating the daily message into your life. The learned behaviors of cynicism, resentment, and getting even are replaced with the skills of Nonviolent Communication, including recognizing one's needs and values and making choices in alignment with them.

Peaceful Living goes beyond daily affirmations, providing the skills and consciousness you need to transform relationships, heal pain, and discover the life-enriching meaning behind even the most trying situations. Begin each day centered and connected to yourself and your values. Direct the course of your life toward your deepest hopes and needs. Ground yourself in the power of compassionate, conscious living.

Available from PuddleDancer Press, the Center for Nonviolent Communication, all major bookstores, and Amazon.com. Distributed by Independent Publisher's Group: 800-888-4741.

About the Author

IKE LASATER, JD, MCP, Author, Mediator, Trainer, and Speaker, helps organizations and individuals increase their conflict navigation skills and the capacity to use those skills in challenging situations. He also acts as a private mediator, facilitating conversations and connection among people in conflict.

A former civil trial attorney, Lasater cofounded a twenty-person law firm, litigating complex, multi-party commercial and environmental cases for twenty years in the state and federal courts of California. He received a master's degree in city planning from the University of California–Berkeley studying global energy policy. Lasater trained extensively with psychologist Marshall B. Rosenberg, PhD, founder of Nonviolent Communication (NVC) for more than a decade, he grew to see that conflict can be an opportunity for connection, and shifted his focus from law to training. NVC's approach was congruent with his values, developed through long-term practices of Zen meditation, yoga (he cofounded *The Yoga Journal* in 1975), and aikido.

Lasater and colleague John Kinyon codeveloped a yearlong immersion training program that is now offered in five countries. (See www.mediate yourlife.com.)

Lasater has served on the boards of directors of the Center for Nonviolent Communication, the Association for Dispute Resolution of Northern California, the California Yoga Teachers Association, The Lawyers Club of San Francisco, the Yale Humanist Community and on the mediation panel for the United States District Court for the Northern District of California.

He has been a guest speaker at Fontys University of Applied Sciences and The HAN University of Applied Sciences in The Netherlands, the University of California–Berkeley, and the Yale School of Management. Lasater has facilitated workshops in more than more than twenty.countries in North and South America, Europe, Africa, Australia, and Asia for such groups as the Dongfeng Nissan car manufacturing plant in Guangzhou, China, BNI in South Korea (with participants from Hyundai and Samsung), Decathlon in Italy, Glynwood in Cold Spring, New York, and in Cleveland, Ohio, the Cleveland Metropolitan Bar Association, The Center for Principled Family Advocacy and The Mediation Association of Northeast Ohio. His mediations include large-scale projects with the University of California–Santa Cruz involving one hundred administrative leaders, and a departmental faculty at the University of California–Los Angeles.

In the wake of the 9/11 attacks, in early 2002, Lasater and his Mediate Your Life cofounder John Kinyon traveled to Afghan refugee camps in Pakistan to offer conflict resolution skills training to elder leaders. And with colleagues at Ayeish, in Spring 2016, he worked with Syrian political opposition leaders of the Etilaf National Coalition of Syrian Revolution and Opposition Forces in Istanbul to offer tools for connection and communication in the midst of intense conflict and negotiation.

For more information about Ike and his work, please visit **ikelasater.com**, where you may also sign up for his mailing list.

You will also find Ike on social media:
Facebook: **facebook.com/IkeLasaterPage**
Twitter: **twitter.com/ikelasater**

To access training videos related to many of the exercises practiced in Ike's workshops, please visit
www.mediateyourlife.com/practice-video-series

Workplace Articles by Ike Lasater

- *New York Times:* What Google Learned From Its Quest to Build the Perfect Team
- *Fast Company*: 3 Ways Companies Are Changing The Dreaded Performance Review
- *Harvard Business Review*: "Fixing Performance Appraisal Is About More than Ditching Annual Reviews"
- *The Library Journal:* "Rethinking the Much-Dreaded Employee Evaluation"
- *Harvard Business Review:* "GE's Real Time Performance Development"
- *Quartz:* Why GE had to kill its annual performance reviews after more than three decades
- *Harvard Business Review:* "Reinventing Performance Management"
- *Fortune:* "IBM Is Blowing Up Its Annual Performance Review"
- *Harvard Business Review:* How to Get Senior Leaders to Change
- *Inc.*: Is Your Leadership Showing?
- *Inc.*: Make a Great First Impression: 7Smart Tricks
- Business Insider: 5 Secrets of Great Bosses
- *Strategic Leadership Studies:* Transformational Leadership
- *Forbes*: Millennials In the Workplace: They Don't Need Trophies But They Want Reinforcement
- *Harvard Business Review:* The Research We've Ignored About Happiness at Work

Books by Ike Lasater

All books are available for purchase on Amazon (Paperback or Kindle).

Collaborating in the Workplace: A Guide for Building Better Teams (Coming Spring 2019)
by Ike Lasater With Julie Stiles

What can individuals do to improve the ability of teams to collaborate and create powerful outcomes? *Collaborating in the Workplace* focuses on the key skills that research shows support effective collaboration and the practical, step-by-step exercises that individuals can practice to improve those skills. By using this book, people can work better together to create outstanding outcomes.

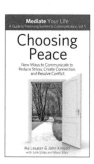

Choosing Peace: New Ways to Communicate to Reduce Stress, Create Connection, and Resolve Conflict
by Ike Lasater and John Kinyon, with Julie Stiles and Mary Sitze

Choosing Peace is about creating inner peace and from that creating peace with others. In it, we give the reader concrete tools with which to do this. It is a practical hands-on book, a relevant and accessible tool for readers no matter their prior familiarity with our work, or Nonviolent Communication.

Book One in the *Mediate Your Life* series, *A Guide to Removing Barriers to Communication.*

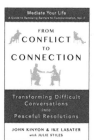

From Conflict to Connection: Transforming Difficult Conversations into Peaceful Resolutions
by Ike Lasater & John Kinyon with Julie Stiles

Everyone experiences conflict, and if you are like most people, it is typically a source of stress or even strife, within relationships. But what if you could have difficult conversations with ease and create agreements that actually work?

With forty years of combined experience in a Nonviolent Communication approach to mediation and conflict resolution, the authors of *From Conflict to Connection* offer a step-by-step guide to being in a relationship with yourself and others that generates new possibilities out of discord and disagreements. If you are ready to escape the power struggle of relationships, be able to hear the other person and express what you would like to say, and find solutions that work for everyone, *From Conflict to Connection* provides a new way forward that has transformed the lives of people worldwide.

Book Two in the *Mediate Your Life* series, *A Guide to Removing Barriers to Communication.*

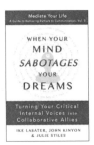

When Your Mind Sabotages Your Dreams: Turning Your Critical Internal Voices Into Collaborative Allies
by Ike Lasater, John Kinyon & Julie Stiles

If you have ever had a dream and then talked yourself out of it, you have experienced internal conflict. The biggest barriers many people face in creating their lives are the self-sabotaging voices that arise within. Learn concrete and practical tools and exercises to mediate internal conflict that will help you stay connected to yourself while you take action to live the life you desire.

Based on the work of *Mediate Your Life*, *When Your Mind Sabotages Your Dreams* is written by authors with nearly 40 years combined experience in a Nonviolent Communication approach to mediation and conflict resolution, who have trained thousands of people worldwide.

Book Three in the *Mediate Your Life* series, *A Guide to Removing Barriers to Communication*.

Mediate Your Life Training Manual, 5th edition
by John Kinyon and Ike Lasater

The *Mediate Your Life* immersion training program supports people in mediating conflict between warring parts of themselves, between self and others, and between others. In three workshops spread over ten months, participants learn to:

- Bring more confidence and ease to dealing with conflict in their lives
- Use the *Mediate Your Life* skills to effectively resolve conflict, heal relationships, and contribute to their own and others' well-being
- Help others who are in conflict

The *Mediate Your Life Training Manual* accompanies the immersion program and includes all of the maps and skills covered in the workshops.

What We Say Matters: Practicing Nonviolent Communication
by Judith Hanson Lasater and Ike Lasater

For yoga teacher Judith Hanson Lasater and mediator Ike K. Lasater, language is a spiritual practice based on giving and receiving with compassion. In *What We Say Matters*, they offer new and nurturing ways of communicating.

Long-term students of yoga and Buddhism, the authors here blend the yoga principle of *satya* (truth) and the Buddhist precept of right speech with Marshall Rosenberg's groundbreaking techniques of Nonviolent Communication (NVC) in a fresh formula for promoting peace at home, at work, and in the world.

The authors offer practical exercises to help readers in any field learn to diffuse anger; make requests rather than demands or assign blame; understand the difference between feelings and needs; recognize how they strategize to get needs met; choose connection over conflict; and extend empathy to themselves and others.